The Eight Powers of a Woman:

Your God-given power to influence the men in your life.

Ja'Ola Walker, D.D.

The Eight Powers of a Woman: Your God-given power to influence the men in your life.
by Ja'Ola Walker, D.D.

Printed in the United States of America

ISBN 978-1-60791-293-4

Unless otherwise indicated, Bible quotations are taken from The King James Version, and The Hebrew-Greek Key Word Study Bible, Copyright © 1984, 1991 by AMG International, Inc. Revised Edition 1991, and The New Strong's Expanded Exhaustive Concordance of the Bible (Red Letter Edition), Copyright © 2001 by Thomas Nelson Publishers, and The Holy Bible: New Living Translation, Copyright © 1996 by Tyndale Charitable Trust, Tyndale House Publishers, Inc Wheaton Illinois 60189, and The Amplified Gospel of John, Copyright © 1954, 1987 by the Lockman Foundation, La Habra, CA 90631, and The Amplified Bible (Mass Market Edition), Copyright © 1965, 1987 by Zondervan Publishing House, Grand Rapids, Michigan 49530, USA, and The Amplified Bible, Old Testament, Part One, Copyright © 1964 by Zondervan Publishing House, Grand Rapids, Michigan 49530, USA, and The Amplified Old Testament, Part Two, Copyright © 1962 by Zondervan Publishing House, Grand Rapids, Michigan 49530, USA , and The Amplified New Testament, Copyright © 1958, 1987 by Zondervan Publishing House, Grand Rapids, Michigan 49530, USA, and The New Revised Standard

Dedicated to the man I love…

You have inspired my life more than you will ever know.
As God took you down into the wells of inspiration,
I was encouraged, blessed and motivated to move to the next level.
You have always set a godly example and
directed me to the light of God's love.

It has been my privilege to be called by God to be your helpmeet.

Special Love and Thanks
goes to
Mom & Dad in Glory

Table of Contents

Foreword

The inspiration for the eight powers of a woman came around 1986 as a result of my study of the Word and my experience as a counselor. I counseled women of various ages and races but most importantly from my personal experience as a husband for 10 years at that time. I began to recognize a God-given power of influence that my wife had in our marriage and I realized how much richer and more effective my life had been as a result of listening to her.

I am who I am today because of her. I have come to appreciate my wife so much more now that I understand these eight powers and God's concept of, "the *ezer*" in Genesis 2:18

Not only women can benefit from understanding these powers but men can be equally blessed. I think the misuse and abuse of women around the world is partly because of the ignorance of both men and women concerning God's purpose and plan for the '*ezer*', the helpmeet.

I am so very excited about my queen's book and the impact that it will have on women throughout the nation and around the world. This is a book idea whose time has come and I am deeply honored and blessed to be married to the author.

Get ready to experience a major paradigm shift in your understanding of who and what a woman is. Get ready for a life changing revelation, get ready to change.

Clarence Walker, PhD
Pastor, Marriage Therapist, Evangelist, Family Life Educator

Introduction

Even in this day and age women still experience discrimination in the church. In nations around the world we are still treated as property, we are still vulnerable in so many ways.

I know how much the Lord loves me and Jesus was so gentle and respectful towards women. Something did not fit. I could feel almost a spiritual negativity against women that seemed universal.

While reading scripture one day a phrase jumped out at me. *Genesis 3:15 And I will put enmity between you and the woman, and between your offspring and hers he will crush your head and you will strike his heel* (NSRV). **If Satan hates us and we hate him maybe that is what I feel in this world.**

I also noticed that Eve was deceived because she wanted power. There are a variety of ways that women try to get power nowadays, some of them are very negative and it sometimes blows up in our face like Eve.

And what in the world is a helpmeet? I found that all of these questions connected and related to each other after my husband began to study the first husband and wife and God's original plan.

Take this journey with me and discover God's plan for us my sister. It is oh so good.

Chapter 1

God's Original Plan for Women

The liberation and fulfillment of woman is not found in the future where we hope and pray that one day, we will finally be affirmed, but it is found at the beginning, in the mind of God. His original plan for women is not restrictive, oppressive or degrading, but liberating and empowering.

Some people have suggested that some of the early church fathers were very negative towards women, but when you look at Scripture and go back to the original plan, you will see the heart of God for His daughters. His plan was for their protection, empowerment and glory.

When women of God understand the nature of the power that has been given to us by God, and how to use that power; that understanding will remedy many problems spiritually, socially and in our relationships. From the beginning of creation, it was evident that we wanted power. However, a lack of understanding of God's original plan has kept power out of our grasp.

Satan could observe several things about Eve as he watched this first couple in the garden. He was looking for a way to destroy them knowing that the only way he could hurt God was to take down the creation that God loved so much.

He noticed how excited Adam was over Eve. She had a lot of influence over him, and she was very curious and more sensitive to the spirit realm. Something about her made Satan think she wanted more, so he decided to tempt her with power.

He was right—she wanted to be like a god knowing good and evil. The serpent put a question in her mind about God. She rehearsed the commandment as relayed to her by Adam, since she wasn't around when God gave it to him. Unfortunately, she added to it saying that they were told not to eat or touch the tree of life. God did not say do not touch it. I think Satan used her presumption, tempted her to touch it, then when she did not immediately die, the foundation was laid to further deceive her. Well, this set up a working relationship between Eve and Satan, and whenever he finds something that works, he works it repeatedly. God steps in and what we have traditionally seen as cursing mankind were really correctives, states Dr. Clarence Walker in his message, "The Naked Truth and The Bare Facts."

It is so important that we understand God's heart about this, my sister. We have all gotten negative messages from birth about our inferiority as women; it is woven into the fabric of our society. If it were just part of one culture, or one time in history, you could discount it. However, there is an undercurrent of antipathy towards women that crosses all cultures, races, and religions. Women carry an inner rage and pain that we have camouflaged, and suppressed for many generations. We all have dreams that have been trampled underfoot just because we were born baby girl Jane rather than baby boy Joe.

Once you get the revelation of God's great love and plan for women, His understanding and gentleness toward us can be seen in the life of Jesus. No wonder Satan has gone out of his way to either make you think you're a nobody or that God thinks less of women. God is preparing a glorious future for His Bride, the church, and He has called you to a bright hope and future. Notice what the Word of God says in Jeremiah 29:11: *"For I know the thoughts that I think toward you, saith the LORD, thoughts of peace, and not of evil, to give you an expected end."*

My prayer is that as you read, the Spirit of the Lord would give you the revelation of the knowledge of His will for your life. I pray that you would see all the power and responsibility He has put in your hands. When our power is misunderstood it is used by Satan to destroy us and those around us. When we operate under the direction of the Holy Spirit, you and I can become powerful weapons of warfare against Satan.

I am defining power as the ability to influence another's behavior. There is power that the Lord gives to all his children. I think God has given women a unique ability to influence the men in our lives …to fulfill a major part of our purpose.

Dr. Clarence Walker (my honey-man) opened my eyes to a revelation of that power when he explained the term "Helpmeet".

The Bible states in Genesis 2:18: *"And the Lord God said, It is not good that the man should be alone: I will make an helpmeet for him." (KJV)*

That leads me to my next chapter, 'What in the world is a helpmeet?'

Chapter 2

What In The World Is A Helpmeet?

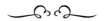

I remember when I first heard the concept of "Ezer" (helpmeet) from my husband. He was sitting in the tub meditating on yet another new revelation God had given him on marriage. This was not unusual for my husband. He is a fountain of amazing revelation. So when he called me into the bathroom to hear this new revelation that the Lord had just dropped in his spirit, my attitude was "yeah, yeah, I'm sure it's great, but I'm busy." However, being the supportive wife that I am, of course I moseyed into the bathroom to listen. He excitedly shared a few paragraphs; I turned, excused myself and **went off.** (In other words I went into spontaneous, totally unexpected high gear praise.) I shouted hallelujah, and wept with joy.

The words he said shot through me like lightning. In a moment this revelation answered unspoken questions, healed unresolved wounds, elevated my image of women back up to where God originally intended us to be. I knew instantly it was from God, a precious jewel from his heart. Here is just a little of what he shared with me that day.

"The term "helpmeet" is one of the terms used in scripture to describe one of the functions of a wife. We are the "ezer", the helpmeet, or the helper suitable. Ezer is the Hebrew word translated helpmeet; it is also one of the functional names of

God. It is mentioned 21 times in scripture and 19 of those times it is referring to God.

*"For example in **Psalm 121:1: "I will lift up mine eyes unto the hills, from whence cometh my <u>help</u>..."** The word help is translated Ezer.*

Psalm 46: 1: "He is very present <u>help</u> in the time of trouble," *again help is translated Ezer."*

"Well if God uses this term to describe Himself it cannot be a term of inferiority. "Women are God's reminder to man that He is committed to help them. Whenever a man looks at his wife, she represents God's help for him. When God wants to get help to the brothers, he will channel it through his wife." God is the big Ezer; she is the little ezer."

Dr. Walker shared that the advantage always goes to the helper; you must have some advantage in order to help someone else. Our senses are more acute, information travels from one side of the female brain to the other side quicker than in the male brain, therefore we talk earlier, and we are able to think about many things at once; we have an intuitiveness that makes us more sensitive to the spiritual realm.

Men think and see the general, the overall picture, in other words, the forest. Women think detailed; we see the specific, the trees in the forest. This difference also qualifies men to better handle being the head; the head must see the overall picture, the forest. The Ezer helps him see the tree that he missed. Eve also had the power to influence Adam. In order to help someone you must also have the ability to influence him.

As women of God we are to use our influence to encourage our husbands towards the will of God. The nature of a helpmeet affects women, whether they are married or not. There are many roles women are expected to play: wife, referee, lover, business administrator, career woman, organizer, mother, chauffeur, homemaker, employee, friend, career counselor, nurse, hostess, cook, den mother, cleaning woman, and on goes the list. You could easily play all these roles in one day, especially if you're a wife and mother.

Out of necessity most women play these roles fairly well. We do all the things nobody else will, and we get practice early in life playing house, feeding dolls, and having tea parties. Many of us had strong role models, mothers who took care of us and everybody else. However, many of us don't understand our God-ordained role. We don't know how we should prioritize our roles, so we are left feeling used, worn out, and unfulfilled.

Let's look back at God's original intention for us:

(God's original intent for woman impacts you whether you are married or not. Therefore, you need to understand this regardless of your marital status.)

Genesis 2:18: *"And the Lord God said, it is not good that the man should be alone; I will make a helpmeet for him."*

1. We were created to be a companion for man. Alone means all one, separated like a branch from a tree.
2. Helpmeet - to help or aid, to surround, protect.

Contrary to traditional thought, God's original plan was that a woman was to play a vital part in a man's life—more than being his cook, baby maker or sex kitten. There is a type of companionship that he can only get from her. You know what happens when you separate a branch from a tree.

There is a way that we protect, surround and help a man. We traditionally think of ourselves as the ones who need protection physically, even emotionally, but there is a certain protection that women provide as well.

Our creation also gives us a clue to our identity...Genesis 2:22: *"and the rib which the Lord God had taken from the man made he a woman."* They were a part of each other. The Bible talks about this great mystery when the two become one flesh in verse twenty-four.

Dr. Clarence identified eight "Ezer powers" that women have been given by God for the purpose of influencing our men towards the will of God. Women have a unique position of influence in a relationship. Influence is power!

If you know how to use your influence you will not have to usurp his authority.

Man has a position of authority given to him by God, and when we usurp (take by force) his authority, we get in trouble with the one who created the system. God did not take away women's ability to influence men. However, after the fall he gave Adam more authority to balance out Eve's influence over him.

You must learn how to use your powers, prioritize your roles, surround, help, and do all of it with a sweet loving attitude! **Does it sound impossible,** like you're expected to be superwoman? Yes, well, without the power of God, it is impossible. The Lord always gives us things to do that are impossible without His help. He always wants you to know that you need Him. The Bible states in **John 15:5:** *"I am the vine ye are the branches.... because apart from me you can do nothing."* (NSRV) The quicker you learn the truth of this verse, the easier your life will be. You cannot be the kind of wife that God requires you to be without His help.

Our God given roles are seen best in the context of marriage, but hang in there single women, the nature of a woman remains whether she is married or not. Understanding these things will help you understand your nature, whether you have a man or not; you operate as a helper to a brother, son, boss, or friend. Certain male/female dynamics are a constant in all opposite sex relationships. **So, let's first look at why God gave you these powers and some of the prerequisites needed before you can fully flow in them.**

Chapter 3

Why I Have These Powers

You need to know why you have these powers and how God intended you to use them. Again, influence is power; a woman who knows how to use her influence will never have to usurp her husband's authority.

Whenever God gives a position of authority or power, there is always responsibility and accountability that go with that power. In every human relationship, where one person can influence another, there is always divine accountability. Teachers influence students, parents influence children, pastors influence their members.

As wives, we are not parenting or pastoring, but we can influence. Eve influenced Adam toward disobedience, destruction and death. Even though she was deceived, she was still held accountable. She suffered the consequences and all of womankind with her.

With each passing day, I realize that being a wife is a calling, just like any other call of ministry, with guidelines, commandments and consequences for disobedience.

Most of us realize we will give an account for our personal lives, but we usually don't include our wifely duties as a part of that judgment. Marriage is not just for you to have a pretty little house in the suburbs and a few children. It is a support system for whatever other areas of ministry you are called to fulfill.

A major part of your purpose as a wife is to influence your husband to fulfill God's will.

While Satan formulated a plan to destroy Adam and Eve, he noticed that Eve had a lot of influence over Adam. At that time they had equal authority, but Eve had more influence. Adam was very excited about her—"bone of my bone, and flesh of my flesh". She was just what the doctor ordered in every way. Satan also noticed that Eve was very intuitive, curious, thirsty for knowledge and more emotional than Adam. He figured if he could trick her, she would use her influence on Adam. Sure enough, Eve was tricked in her attempt to get more knowledge and be a god.

Genesis 3:5 says: *"For God doth know that in the day ye eat thereof, then your eyes shall be opened, and ye shall be as gods, knowing good and evil."* She then used her verbal power to convince Adam. He was not deceived; he was influenced. Genesis 3:17 says: *"And unto Adam he said, Because thou hast hearkened unto the voice of thy wife, and hast eaten of the tree, of which I commanded thee, saying, Thou shalt not eat of it: cursed is the ground for thy sake; in sorrow shalt thou eat of it all the days of thy life."* The word "hearken" in the original language means to hear intelligently with attention and obedience. The word "voice" means to call aloud, crackling, proclaim, thundering voice, to yell.

Girlfriend did not just sweetly try to influence Adam, but she used one of her powers of influence—her mouth. Eve messed up. She knew it and since misery loves company, she yelled, fussed and thundered until Adam gave in.

This man who had walked with God daily on an intimate level, who flowed in a loving relationship with God, gave it all up to please his wife. **He chose the door that said death.**

Whenever we choose to obey someone rather than God, we make that person an idol. Adam made Eve his god. She got her wish for a moment; however, it blew up in her face.

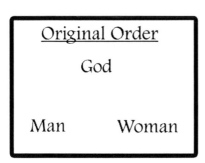

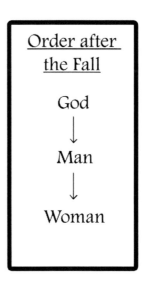

God rearranged the authority hierarchy; He put Adam to rule over Eve.

Dr. Clarence Walker talks about three correctives to balance the amount of influence that Eve had on Adam in his message, "The Naked Truth and the Bare Facts." After the fall into sin, with the amount of influence Eve had over Adam, her disregard for life, the easy way Satan could deceive her, and her advantages over Adam; if God didn't do something Eve and Satan would have run the planet.

Dr. Walker describes the original plan that God has for man and woman as the "Creative Roles", the changes that sin brought into their relationship, were their "Conflictive Roles". God made changes in their relationship after the fall; these are their "Corrective Roles". Let's look at the changes.

1. **Change of the power hierarchy—Adam will now rule over Eve, her desire towards her husband always brings her back in check.**
2. **Eve was now assigned pain in childbirth, she showed a lack of respect for life, which would now be corrected as she struggled in pain to bring it forth.**

3. **Adam would now have to struggle to eat and bring life from the ground, it was cursed due to him. (Gen 3:16-19) Work became a distraction from Eve.**
4. **God puts hatred between Eve and the serpent to break up their alliance. (Gen 3:15) It would be her seed (Jesus) that would be Satan's destroyer.**

God specifically cursed the ground and the serpent. The serpent was cursed, because he deceived Eve and led her into sin. The actual animal was cursed above all the livestock and all the wild animals. He would crawl on his belly and eat dust all the days of his life. To the spiritual serpent, Satan, God declared his future destruction to come through the seed of the woman. **Genesis 3:15:** *"And I will put enmity between thee and the woman, and between thy seed and her seed; it shall bruise thy head, and thou shalt bruise his heel."* The seed of the woman is Jesus, born of the virgin who would ultimately destroy the head or power base of Satan at Calvary. God also decided to break up this little alliance that Eve and the serpent had formed.

He Hates Us!

God took the very creature Satan used to attack mankind (Eve) to attack him back. From this point forward there would be a God-given enmity (strong hatred) between Satan and the woman.

We have seen through the ages that Satan has a particular hatred for women. It has expressed itself in all the cruelties that women have endured for generations. For many ages and even until today, in some places women are considered the property of a man, to be used, discarded, and raped. She had little or no rights in government, many times not being allowed to vote nor considered a citizen in full standing. If she doesn't have a husband or a father to protect her, she is fair game. This contempt, distrust, disregard and even hatred seen throughout history did not come from men, even though they are usually the vessels and agents through which it is expressed.

This Hatred Comes From Satan

This hatred in all its filthy persistent cruelty comes from the very pit of hell. That's why it crosses color lines, time lines, and educational lines, in every country, age, and culture. The hatred comes from Satan; it has been around as long as he has because he fuels it. Instead of a Women's Movement, we need to start a "Hate Satan Movement." His hatred for us is seen in society, culture and history.

In Jesus' day, women could not study scripture; they were not counted or numbered in a crowd. The early church fathers considered them evil distractions; this was the historical basis for the priests taking a vow of celibacy. This leaves us as women in a society that hates us; we are easy prey, raped and abused, beaten up by husbands, sexually harassed by bosses and preyed upon by wicked leaders.

We still have fewer rights and job opportunities, the statistics of incest are blowing the minds of sociologists, and most violent crimes are committed against women. Rock music videos combine violence and sex leading young men to think they go together. Date rape is on the rise. Therefore, you have another generation of men coming up who are being trained to use and abuse.

There are increasing reports of young men who get obsessed with a girl, and then they will stalk and torment these young girls if they decide to date someone else and in some cases these young men have gotten violent. Even today I have been in churches where I was bringing the message but not allowed to stand in the pulpit – I had to minister from the choir stand. Some ministers think we are 'unclean'. However, men are not the enemy; the hatred goes back to Satan. He fuels the violence.

This negativity did not come from God. Biblically, women have a very honorable place in the heart of God. We were also created in the image of God.

Genesis 1:27: *"...in the image of God he created them, male and female he created them."* The Genesis picture of the relationship between the man and woman before the fall was what God originally intended for them. They were to reflect the image of God, multiply and fill the earth with sons of God, take authority and subdue the enemy together.

Jesus treated women with much love and respect. He honored and lifted women to a new spiritual height, even going against the public opinion and tradition of the times. He commended a black woman on her faith; He stopped to talk to a Samaritan woman with bad morals. He shared with her some of the most revealing and important teaching about God and worship. Jesus showed a new kind of love and patience for women as He encouraged Mary for wanting to learn spiritual truths, in a culture where women were not even allowed to read the scripture.

With the creation of the Body of Christ, God declared through Paul that "In Christ", in the spiritual realm, there is neither male nor female, Jew nor Greek. (Galatians 3:28) These areas where we discriminate against each other in the natural world, do not apply in the spiritual realm. **Woman, you can be a five star general in God's army, if you are willing to pay the price.**

Way down on the inside of each of us is a built in hatred for that old serpent, Satan, who deceived our first sister, Eve, so long ago. We have to get past blaming our problems on everyone else, especially men, open our spiritual eyes and see the source of the arrows, spears and missiles that are coming at us.

We wrestle not against flesh and blood but against the kingdom of darkness. God also let Satan know at that time that a seed would be coming from the woman who would ultimately destroy him by crushing his head. How do you kill a serpent? Crush his head!

This was the first promise of a Savior, who would come virgin born, through the womb and destroy Satan. He began to watch more closely the seed, the children; wondering when this 'one' would come to destroy him. He probably watched how Abel was obedient to God and motivated Cain's jealousy and murder. Several times when he got nervous about this special seed coming, he would get in the heart of the king, or ruler to kill all the boy babies, so he could wipe out the seed early in the game.

- To the woman God said *He would greatly increase her pain and sorrow in childbearing, her desire would be to her husband, and he would rule over her.*
- To Adam, God said: because you listened to your wife instead of me, cursed is the ground because of you, and you will have to sweat and struggle to live. (This was to counterbalance the influence that Eve had on him. Work gave him a new focus.) Also He would die and return to the dust he came from.

God put some limitations on Eve's influence by setting up some conditions that would dilute that influence, but he still left her that power. There were also some other natural and spiritual results of God's correctives and curses. The pain in childbirth helped Eve to have an appreciation for life and develop her maternal instinct.

Secondly, her desire would now be toward her husband. Genesis 3:16: *"Unto the woman he said, I will greatly multiply thy sorrow and thy conception; in sorrow thou shalt bring forth children; **and thy desire shall be to thy husband, <u>and he shall rule over thee.</u>**"*

The Hebrew word for "desire" is *teshuwqah* [1] it means a stretching out after; a longing, and a part of that word is shuwq [2] which means to run after or over. As women, we have the desire **to stretch out and long for a man,** and we <u>**desire to run after them and over them.**</u> These conditions set in motion some conditions that we must deal with until this day.

Notes:

1. The New Strong's Expanded Exhaustive Concordance of the Bible (Red Letter Edition) Copyright©2001 by Thomas Nelson Publishers. The Hebrew and Aramaic Dictionary. Page 303
2. Ibid. The Hebrew and Aramaic Dictionary. Page 275

Chapter 4

The Eight *Ezer* Powers

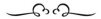

Y ou need to understand the influence you have with men and how to use it properly. All women have this influence, whether you are married or not, whether you understand it or not.

My prayer is that the Spirit of the Lord would give you the revelation of the power and responsibility He has put in your hands. When our power is misunderstood, it is used by Satan to destroy us and those around us. When we operate under the direction of the Holy Spirit, you and I can become a powerful weapon of harassment and warfare against Satan.

As women of God we are to use our influence to push our husbands towards the will of God.

The nature of a helper suitable affects all women. Whoever you are, there is a man somewhere (father, brother, friend, husband, boss) who has a need, problem, or weakness. He is stuck and has gone as far as he can on his own. He needs help to go on. Man always has to go pass a woman.

He passes **through** his mother, passes **by** his sister and passes **with** his wife.

Rahab helped the spies and Joshua; she was a harlot who helped and ended up in the hall of fame (Hebrews 11).

The widow helped Elijah and became a successful entrepreneur.

The virtuous woman got praise from God, her husband, and her children.

The failure of Eve was that she used her influence and power to pull him into destruction. The Lord said to Eve, your desire shall be to your husband, and he shall rule over thee. That is the problem ladies, no matter how independent we get, how much money we make, we have an emotional need. We want a man to hold us at the end of the day.

We are always tempted to run after them but due to our abilities we are also tempted to run over them.

We have some advantages: you know that while he is at point A, B, and C, our quick minds have already gone to Z and back. They miss details that we pick up because that is the way God made us – Men see the forest, women see the trees.

We are rebellious by nature – so God tells us to submit.

All you single ladies who want a man but don't seem to realize that you are being called to a life of submission; you're the most rebellious thing on the block.

Eve influenced Adam toward disobedience, the devil, destruction, and death, and even though she was deceived, she was still held accountable by God and she suffered the consequences.

When man is left alone, man becomes self-focused, self-absorbed, self-contained and self-centered. That is why it is not good for man to be alone. Therefore, God made a helper suitable. Women are God's earthly facilitators, channels of divine aid.

You see these powers to influence even when your little three-year-old daughter bats her eyes at her daddy, she is learning to influence.

I give my precious husband credit for hearing this revelation from God. Remember, all of these powers can be used for good or evil.

Eight Ezer Powers

1. <u>Distributional Power – The power of giving</u>

The Biblical example was Eve dealing with Adam. *Genesis 3:6: "She gave also unto her husband and he did eat."* Giving is one of the woman's powers. We are always in a giving role with our families. We give time, energy, talents, skills, love, hope, encouragement, and our passion. Your giving is the heart of your home, and you are probably the core that holds it all together.

We instinctively know that there is power in giving because when we are angry and want revenge, we stop giving. Wives stop giving intimacy, dinner, cleaning, and loving.

Many men who have extra-marital affairs have said that it was not about how the other woman looked, it was the giving, the sharing, how the other woman made him feel.

2. Paradoxical Power – the power of paradox
The Biblical example is Sarai and Abraham.

Genesis 16:1-6: "Now Sarai Abram's wife bare him no children: And Sarai said unto Abram, Behold now, the LORD hath restrained me from bearing: I pray thee, go in unto my maid; it may be that I may obtain children by her. And Abram hearkened to the voice of Sarai."

She told Abraham to take the concubine, then turned around and blamed him. Women can often contradict themselves. This does not compute with the brothers shorting out their mental computers. They end up giving in. We think with both sides of our brain at the same time. Sometimes one side of your brain will contradict the other. For example, when my husband asks if I want something from the store, and I tell him no, but once he comes back eating goodies I will ask, "You didn't bring me anything? You know I didn't mean no." This is very frustrating to men.

"Ok, ok whatever you want." They placate you to get peace. Peace is very important to men.

3. Verbal power – The power of words – the example is of Delilah:
I bet you thought Delilah seduced Samson. Armies could not take him down, he was the strongest man in the world, but a little woman took him down. It wasn't her seduction, but her mouth.

The Bible says in Judges 16:16: *"And it came to pass, when she pressed him daily with her words, and urged him, so that his soul was vexed unto death."*

Life and death are in the power of the tongue – you can bring life to the people around you or you can be a tool of destruction in the devil's hand.

The Bible says in Proverbs 12: 4: *"A virtuous woman is a crown to her husband: but she that maketh ashamed is as rottenness in his bones."* (Ouch – the Word can be tough!)

When we shame them with our words, it actually affects their health. The nagging, fussing, emasculating, cruel, biting words rot their bones.

The Bible says in Proverbs 15:1: *"A soft answer turns away wrath, but a harsh word stirs up anger. The tongue of the wise dispenses knowledge but the mouths of fools pour out folly."*

4. <u>**Maternal Power – The power of womanhood**</u> – Our Biblical example is Hannah.

The Bible says in I Samuel 1:22-23: *"But Hannah went not up; for she said unto her husband, I will not go up until the child be weaned, and then I will bring him, that he may appear before the Lord, and there abide forever. And Elkanah her husband said unto her, Do what seemeth thee good; tarry until thou have weaned him; only the Lord establish his word."*

Many times men will do things for the benefit of their children when they will not move for anything else. The mother's heart can appeal to the father for the sake of their children.

5. <u>**Reverential Power – The Power of Reverence**</u> **– Our Biblical example is Abigail -** The Bible says in I Samuel 25:23: *"And when Abigail saw David, she hasted, and lighted off the ass, and fell before David on her face, and bowed herself to the ground, And fell at his feet, and said, Upon me, my lord, upon me let this iniquity be: and let thine handmaid, pray thee, speak in thine audience, and hear the words of thine handmaid."*

Abigail was married to a fool who had insulted King David, and David was going to kill everybody because of it. She ran out to meet him to intercede for her husband. She brought a gift (distributional power) and then she reverenced him as king – she called him Lord 14 times. She gave him a wise plan, and he spared Nabal's life. She impressed David so much that later after her husband died, David went back and married her.

Learn how to respect authority—first God, then the systems He sets up. He will fight on your behalf when you honor him.

The opposite of reverencing the authority systems that God sets up is rebellion—the extreme of that is witchcraft.

6. Regal Power – The power of Queenly honor – Our Biblical Example is Esther

The Bible says in Esther 5:1: *"Now it came to pass on the third day, that Esther put on her royal apparel, and stood in the inner court of the king's house, over against the king's house: and the king sat upon his royal throne in the royal house, over against the gate of the house."*

The Bible says in Esther 5:2: *"And it was so, when the king saw Esther the queen standing in the court, that she obtained favour in his sight: and the king held out to Esther the golden scepter that was in his hand. So Esther drew near, and touched the top of the scepter."*

The Bible says in Esther 5:3: *"Then said the king unto her, what wilt thou, Queen Esther? And what is thy request? It shall be even given thee to the half of the kingdom."*

Sometimes when you recognize the queen in you and carry yourself with queenly dignity, your king recognizes his queen. Dress the part. Improve your self confidence. You need to say what God says about you.

- *I am fearfully and wonderfully made. I am a royal priest. The Lord beautifies me. He is renewing the years that the locust and cankerworm have eaten. My youth is being renewed like the eagle. I have the mind of Christ.*

Nothing is more attractive than a woman who feels good about herself and looks her best.

7. <u>**Sensual Power –The Power of Allurement**</u> – **Our Biblical example is Salome**

The Bible says in Mark 6:22: *"And when the daughter of the said Herodias came in, and danced, and pleased Herod and them that sat with him, the king said unto the damsel, Ask of me whatsoever thou wilt, and I will give it thee."*

Salome used her sensuality to get what she wanted, she danced and worked those hips and thighs until the man promised her up to half of his kingdom.

Women of God should not be using this power to seduce; only wives should be using this power. Everything about you is to comfort your husband, but don't use it as a weapon.

It is fine to be sensual, seductive and passionate with **your** husband. God put that passion in you. It is not bad. Sex was God's idea. Stop being corny girl, and go get you some sexy night gowns. Your husband is stimulated by sight. Be his eye candy.

8. <u>**Prophetical Power – The Power of Intuition**</u> – **Our Biblical example is Pilate's wife**

The Bible says in Matthew 27:19: *"When he was set down on the judgment seat, his wife sent unto him, saying, Have thou nothing to do with that just man: for I have suffered many things this day in a dream because of him."*

The more you open your spirit to the Lord, the more He will give you dreams, and sensitivity to the Spirit. He will lead you to pray about certain things. We have that intuition that can be used in a positive way.

Of all these powers, ladies, verbal power is one of the most important. Life and death are in the power of the tongue. All of the *Ezer* powers can be used under the influence of the Holy Spirit or the direction of Satan and your sin nature.

One of the most important tools is your tongue. Let's learn how to use our tongues as instruments of life.

Chapter 5

The Power of the Tongue

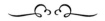

Women in general have a problem with their tongues. Much of what Solomon addresses to women in Proverbs concerns her tongue. We are associated with backbiting, gossiping, being busy-bodies and being talkative.

As an African American woman, I know that sisters in particular have perfected the technique and developed their own style that is recognized throughout the world. We have even developed body movement and expressions to add strength to our presentation.

Nobody can tell you off like a sister. However, we must all realize that life and death are in the power of the tongue. Whether we are speaking to our husbands, our children or each other, we have the power to pour out death or pour out life.

If you realize that there have been times that you have used your tongue in a negative way (we all have), for there to be real change, we must get to the root of the problem. You can't just grit your teeth and talk nice. It has to be in your heart. You can't put on a false smile and say, 'oh, dear, I'm proud of you', when in your heart you're really saying, 'this dumb fool does not know what he's doing'. He'll get the message from your heart in spite of your words.

God wants to deal with the root of the problem, because what is in your heart, your mouth will speak. The Word tells us that out of the abundance of the heart the mouth speaketh.

There are four main root sins that affect our mouths:

1. Pride   2. Anger   3. Bitterness   4. Fear

From these four come others: hurt, resentment, rebellion, self hate and others.

Different women have different root sins that can be manifested in the same way.

The first root sin is Pride, which leads to rebellion. This woman uses her tongue as an expression of her rebellion.

"Nobody tells me what to do; you are not my father." Rebellious lips are proud lips.

Psalm 12:3, 4: *"The Lord shall cut off all flattering lips and the tongue that speaketh proud things, who have said with our tongues, we will prevail, our lips are our own, who is lord over us?"*

The Bible says in Proverbs 28:25: *"He that is of a proud heart stirreth up strife."*

The Bible says in I Samuel 15:23: *"For rebellion is as the sin of witchcraft."*

A woman with a proud heart causes dissension. She is self-righteous, critical, boastful, and disrespectful to authority. She looks for alternatives to submission. "I have the same Holy Ghost he has. This is a body ministry, why do we have to listen to the Pastor"?

She can be the bossy mother type who is confrontive and in your face. She will just tell you up front that you are a fool and don't know what you are talking about. Then you have the condescending mother type. She talks down to everyone, no one knows as much, and it is hard for her to learn from others.

Both mother types are damaging to the male ego.

The Second Root Sin is Anger:

The Bible says in Proverbs 21:19: *"It is better to dwell in the wilderness, than with a contentious and an angry woman."*

The Bible says in Proverbs 29:21, 23: (NIV) *"Under three things the earth trembles, under four it cannot bear up, a servant who becomes king, a fool who is full of food, An unloved woman who is married."*

This woman is angry and hurt, her needs are not met and her expectations are dashed. She can be that raving maniac, throwing things and talking violently. In an argument she goes for the juggler. Women who are prone towards anger have a tendency to cover their hurt with anger. She feels unloved, neglected and criticized. Many of us carried our hurts over into our Christian life and just put a spiritual label on wounds that we have never gotten healed. I've heard women say, "I'm a prophet" but they were just using the pulpit to lay everybody out.

The third root sin is bitterness: Bitterness begins with hurt that is internalized.

The Bible says in Hebrews 12:15: *"Look diligently lest any man fail of the grace of God lest any root of bitterness springing up trouble you and thereby many be defiled."*

The hurt turns to resentment and bitterness which wrap around our insides like a root. It affects our thoughts, and opinions about everything. "Honey, all men are alike, they use you and leave you."

Bitterness can also be manifest in a more subtle way. Some women are very quiet, but once they speak, their words can cut like a sword. This woman never forgets an offense. Your thought life can be full of bitterness and anger that you just don't have the courage to express. It is better to deal with your hurt and speak the truth in love. The Bible tells us that anger rests in the bosom of fools. When we let it sit in our hearts it turns to bitterness and poisons us.

Don't hold it all in; one day you may snap and ruin your life with a foolish act.

<u>The fourth root sin is fear.</u> The woman with this root is usually a worrier, a complainer, and a nagger. She has a fear of losing, is full of insecurities, and strikes out at others first to protect herself. She plays big and bad so no one will mess with her. On the inside she is a fearful little girl.

Other women have a lot of self hate, so they spend their lives criticizing others. "Did you see that ugly, tacky dress? She thinks she's cute". This is a common phrase of women with insecurities and poor self images. They must pull others down to feel good about themselves.

Our first step is to allow the Lord to put a finger on the root sin in our lives that is overflowing out of our mouths.

Some of us need inner healing from those open wounds in our soul. Others need an understanding of God's love to remove that self hate. You might need to allow God to take away that spirit of fear, pride and rebellion. Allow God to deal with your spirit of unforgiveness.

You may still be angry with your father. Perhaps he abused you, but you will not be free until you choose to forgive and release him. Even if he has died, you must forgive and receive inner healing. A good Christian counselor can help you through a process of healing.

You might dress up, get degrees, become sophisticated, or do church work but that root of bitterness will defile you; just like the roots of a tree that wraps around everything near it. You may have a good reason to be angry and bitter, and I am sure you could tell some sad stories. However, the bottom line is, if you do not forgive that person, the situation continues to hurt and destroy you by bringing you into bondage. You will remember and experience the pain over and over and the root grows and blocks out meaningful relationships with people and hinders your relationship with God.

Bitterness causes you to be angry, depressed and discouraged. Forgiving is for **your** sake.

The second principle is that life and death are in the power of the tongue. (Proverbs 18:21)

Women, we need to realize how much God can use us to heal our people. This is the same instrument that Satan has used to criticize, emasculate and demoralize our men, children and each other. God wants to use you to bring healing to people.

Let's look at the negative forces in the tongue:

1st Negative Force – The Tongue Can Defile the Whole Body

The Bible says in James 3:6-8: *"And the tongue is a fire. The tongue is placed among our members as a world of iniquity; it stains the whole body, sets on fire the cycle of nature and is itself set on fire by hell. For every species of beast and bird, of reptile and sea creature, can be tamed and has been tamed by the human species, but no one can tame the tongue—a restless evil, full of deadly poison."*

2nd Negative Force – Words Can Cause Wounds that go Down into Your Inner Being

The Bible says in Proverbs 18:8: "The words of a whisperer are like delicious morsels; they go down into the inner parts of the body." (AMP)

The Bible says in Proverbs 12:18: "Rash words are like sword thrusts, but the tongue of the wise brings healing." (NSRV)

Many of us experienced this in childhood, words that were spoken to us that we incorporated into our psyche; it becomes a part of us. "You're ugly, you're dumb, worthless" or you may have heard, "all men are dogs, all Jews are…, all blacks are…" You may have even bought into the lies about God.

Don't make the same mistakes with your children. To some of us it is just habit, we heard our mothers speak a certain way and we model after them. Even sometimes when you say, "I'll never do it like my mother did," you find the same words, attitudes and ideas coming out of your mouth.

3rd Negative Force – Words Can Stir Up Anger

The Bible says in Proverbs 15:1-2: *"A soft answer turns away wrath, but a harsh word stirs up anger. The tongue of the wise dispenses knowledge but the mouths of fools pour out folly."*

4th Negative Force – Words can wound a Spirit

The Bible says in Proverbs 15:4: *"A gentle tongue is a tree of life, but perverseness in it breaks the spirit."*

5th Negative Force –Words Can Break up Friendships

The Bible says in Proverbs 16:28: *"A perverse person spreads strife, and a whisperer separates close friends."*

6th Negative Force— Your Words Can Destroy & Trap You

The Bible says in Proverbs 18:7: *"The mouths of fools are their ruin, and their lips a snare to themselves."*

The Bible says in Proverbs 13:3 *"Those who guard their mouths preserve their lives; those who open wide their lips come to ruin."* (NSRV)

The Bible also talks about women who have learned to use this force in a more subtle way.

The Bible says in Proverbs 6:24: *"To keep thee from the evil woman, from the flattery of the tongue of a strange woman."*

The Bible says in Proverbs 7:5: *"That they may keep thee from the strange woman, from the stranger which flattereth with her words."*

Flattery means to be smooth, to divide.

The Bible says in Proverbs 7:21: *"With her much fair speech she caused him to yield, with the flattering of her lips she forced him."*

Proverbs 7:10 talks about a woman, who the Bible says is a harlot. We do not think we are harlots but many 'Christian' women fit the description.

She is loud, stubborn; her feet abide not in her house. The Bible says in Proverbs 9:13: *"A foolish woman is clamorous, loud, she is simple, and knoweth nothing."*

Our words are very important to God, you can lay me out and forget about it and move on but your words are lasting and note-worthy to God.

1. **Words are being recorded**—Matt 12: 36: "But I say unto you, that every idle word that men shall speak, they shall give account thereof in the Day of Judgment."

The Bible says in Malachi 3:16: ***"Then they that feared the LORD spake often one to another: and the LORD hearkened, and heard it, and a book of remembrance was written before him for them that feared the LORD, and that thought upon his name."***

2. **Words will be an important yardstick for God's judgment.**

The Bible states in Matthew 12:37: "For by thy words thou shalt be justified, and by thy words thou shalt be condemned."

Now let's look at the four positive forces we have in our tongues:

1. **Words can be sweet and actually affect a person's health.**

The Bible says in Proverbs 16:24: "Pleasant words are as an honeycomb, sweet to the soul, and health to the bones."

The Bible says in Proverbs 12:18: "There is that speaketh like the piercings of a sword: but the tongue of the wise is health."

The Bible says in Proverbs 15:4: "A wholesome tongue is a tree of life: but perverseness therein is a breach in the spirit."

Wholesome means curative, literally a medicine, a remedy.

Some husbands may have ulcers and high blood pressure due to their wife's mouth.

The Bible says in Proverbs 19:13: *"… and the contentions of a wife are a continual dropping."*

You know that continual nagging? We all probably felt like our mothers nagged us as teenagers. It would drive you crazy. Men have an even lower tolerance for nagging. If it worked that would be different, but it doesn't. Nagging leaves you mad and your husband turned off, so let's find something that works.

The 2nd Positive Force in the tongue – Your words can bring peace into an angry situation.

The Bible says in Proverbs 15:1: "A soft answer turneth away wrath: but grievous words stir up anger."

Our anger inflames his. We try to use anger to make our point. Some of us can't confront unless we're angry. You don't make a point when you're angry. When no one is listening the person puts up their defenses. It's wasted energy, stop wasting your energy and emotions on things that do not accomplish what you want. Some of you need to stop arguing and get on your knees, which is where the power is to effect change. You can fuss all day, but it does not bring about a lasting change.

If you're angry, channel that emotion towards the devil; he's your real enemy.

The Bible says in Ephesians 6:12: "For we wrestle not against flesh and blood, but against principalities, against powers, against the rulers of the darkness of this world, against spiritual wickedness in high places."

3. Your words can bring wisdom and knowledge to a person.

The Bible says in Proverbs 10:31: "The mouth of the righteous brings forth wisdom." (NSRV)

The Bible states in Proverbs 16:21: "The wise of heart is called perceptive, and pleasant speech increases persuasiveness."

This principle blew my mind that we can increase learning in others by our words. Do you think that man is dumb? Are your children having problems in school? You're probably telling that man that he is dumb, and increasing your children's mental block with criticism.

Try this principle – not flattery, but positive, encouraging, supportive words.

The Bible states in **Proverbs 16:21** (Amplified) – The wise in heart shall be called prudent, understanding and knowing and winning speech increases learning in both speaker and listener.

(NIV)…pleasant words promote instruction and make a man persuasive.

The Proverbs 31 woman opened her mouth with wisdom and in her tongue was the law of kindness.

4. Your words can build torn down situations.

The Bible states in Proverbs 11:13: *"A gossip goes about telling secrets, but one who is trustworthy in spirit keeps a confidence."* (NRSV)

Faithful spirit means to build up or support, to foster as a parent or nurse.

The Bible states in Proverbs 14:1: *"The wise woman¹ builds her house, but the foolish tears it down with her own hands."* (NRSV)

Now let's look at 5 principles to govern our tongue:

1) **Shut up** – some of us talk day and night, nonstop and we all need to talk much less. When you realize what a powerful tool your tongue is you don't want to waste your time with idle, useless words that accomplish nothing.

The Bible states in Proverbs 13:3: *"...he that openeth wide his lips shall have destruction."*

Some of you brag about speaking your mind, but according to the Word that is not wise.

The Bible states in Proverbs 18:28: *"The heart of the righteousness studieth to answer; but the mouth of the wicked poureth out evil things."*

Think about "how will this affect him? Will it accomplish what I want? Will it make him feel insecure?"

The Bible states in Proverbs 15:2: *"The tongue of the wise useth knowledge aright; but the mouth of fools poureth out foolishness."*

2) **Get information first – Proverbs 18:13:** *"He that answereth a matter before he heareth it, it is folly and shame unto him."*

Have you ever put your foot in your mouth before you got all the facts and then felt like a fool once you heard the whole story?

3) **Ask the Lord to set a watch over your mouth** (Psalms 141:3). Be like David who asked the Lord to keep the door of

his lips. Now when you ask the Lord to set a watch, He will and when you feel the tug of the Holy Spirit it is up to you to yield to him. We all have had times when we felt the Lord warning us to be quiet, but we waved Him off and said, "No Holy Ghost, I've got to tell this man off". Unfortunately, you pay the price when you don't obey.

4) **Allow the Word to become a part of you.** The Word of God is the Word of life, wisdom and power. As you read, study, meditate and memorize it, it will take root within you and come out of your mouth.

Those four words are different. The first is **read** -we should read the Word, but that's different from study. **Study** includes a pencil, paper, study helps, a background, and history, the meaning of the words, comparing verses, and reading other versions. If you don't know how to do this on your own, go to Bible School, or get a book on how to study the Bible. There are many resources. The next word is **meditate** which means; to mull it over in your mind, think on it, and apply it to your life.

The fourth word is **memorize** - memorize verses that will help you in your weak areas, use them when you are down. Use them as a weapon on Satan.

5) **Try to think & speak positively.** The word tells you whatsoever things are pure, honest and of good report, think on these things.

Think and dwell on the positive things. What is in your heart and mind will come out of your mouth. Even the best man is not good enough if you are always picking him apart and focusing on the negative. Even Superman would fall short. Mrs. Superman would probably ask, "What's up with the cape man?"

Pick out the positive and talk about it. Instead of running the man down to your friend, speak and think the positive.

Understand the importance of the male ego. It is crucial to deal with a man, that's what puts the starch in his backbone.

If your man has a damaged ego and feels powerless in this society you must use your tongue as a remedy, a medicine to build up what has been torn down.

Now I know you may say, "I don't want to go through all those changes guarding my words, handling some man with kid gloves, he's the man, he should be stronger."

There are some men with a good self image, secure about who they are, ambitious, independent and responsible. However, there are others who are wounded and did not have a proper role model. If you learn to see potential in people regardless of his weakness, God has a purpose for him to be a mighty man.

It takes the right woman (and the help of the Holy Ghost) to make a good man a great man. That is a major part of your job as the Helpmeet. A wise woman will use her tongue as a powerful tool of life under the control of the Holy Spirit. Learn to see positive potential and build and encourage it with your tongue.

When I was first married my husband was not a handy man. He was a brainy guy who didn't know how to fix anything. We would always call his stepfather for the little repairs in the house. Well, one day we couldn't get his stepfather, so I said to my husband, "Sweetheart, you are a brilliant man I believe you can fix this faucet." "Oh you think I can do it?" he asked. I responded, "I know you can do it, baby."

You've got to learn how to work that mouth girlfriend. My husband went on to fix the faucet, he put a new floor on my kitchen, he paneled the hallway, and he lowered the ceiling in the bedroom. He did an excellent job; he had talents that he never realized.

Make a list of all his positive characteristics. The Lord wants to use you as the Helpmeet to make him the man he should be, but the Devil wants to use you to destroy him. (A wise woman buildeth her house but the foolish woman plucketh it down with her own hands) Many times the other woman is only picking up the pieces that you have already torn down with your own actions, words and attitudes.

When you find your man on the defensive, you can tell when he starts talking stupid. That is the time that your speech and attitude must help him to come off the defensive.

When he starts blaming you and others; denying or changing the subject, he is on the defense. It's time to back off, get quiet, and bring it up at another time. Check your attitude, be sure that you are not attacking, and apologize. Take your part of the blame; it will help him accept his part of the problem. Put yourself in his shoes, how would it affect you?

I had a young lady call me one day. She had been arguing with her husband for a while. She wanted me to talk to him on the phone and tell him he was wrong. I asked her to think how would she respond if he did that to her.

Statements like, "you're so dumb, you don't know how to fix anything" would put anyone on the defensive. Even if you don't say those words, if you talk down to him, and he reads it in your attitude it still has the same effect.

Giving orders will put him on the defensive. Men have a fear of being dominated by women. Instead of saying do this and do that, ask, "Sweetheart would you please do this? Do you think you have time? Could you possibly?"

Ask a question rather than give a command. Give him basic respect. He is not your son. If you tear him down he will not be the strong man you need him to be.

Use those positive names: sweetheart, honey, baby, sugar. They will help you remember to be positive. No one says, "Sweetheart, go jump off a bridge."

Do not use negative names like fool, stupid, dumb and so forth.

These are all things to prevent you from speaking positively.

What happens when you are angry, he is on your last nerve, you are ready to 'cuss' him out?

1. If possible, take a break from the situation. Ask to talk about it later. Let him know you need to cool off. Cool off, vent to the Lord, and tell Him about it. Pray and then try to go back and talk through it.

2. Allow your love to guard you. Know that once you've said it you can never take it back. Your words can make a wound that will never heal and like a scab they build walls that will come between you. Some couples are like strangers in the night, roommates with no intimacy or closeness.

3. Confront the action never the person's character. It is better to say, "I don't like it when you do...." Do not say, "You are so stupid to do that." Deal with the action not the person's character.

Relationships are work. This is not the 'Love Boat' or a romance novel. The reality is Satan hates godly relationships, and he will fight against you. However, greater is He that is in you. Jesus died for you to walk in victory. Yield unto God. Satan has no power over you unless you give in to the flesh.

There are principles of life in the Word of God. Use God's principles rather than just doing what you were taught or saw.

God is raising up a new generation of women that have power in their mouths to heal, encourage, strength, soothe, inspire and declare the Word of God. You choose.

Chapter 6

Your Father Wants You to Have Even More Power

There are powers that we have in the natural, but **God wants to give His daughters some spiritual power.**

God is looking for vessels to show Himself strong through. He wants to give out power, but the higher levels of power are reserved for those who walk in obedience. The more obedient you are, the more power you will walk in.

Women, you are called, destined, and ordained to walk in the power of God.

The Bible says in Luke 10:19: "Behold, I give unto you [1]**power** to tread on serpents and scorpions, and over all the [2]**power** of the enemy: and nothing shall by any means hurt you." There are two Greek words for power in this verse.

The first word for power in that verse came from the Greek word (Exousia) which means privilege, force, capacity, competency, superhuman ability. The second word power in that verse comes from the Greek word (dunamis) which means force, miraculous power, ability, violence and mighty. Therefore, when you put that together with those meanings it reads like this: *"Behold, I give unto you privilege, force, capacity, competency and superhuman ability to tread on serpents and scorpions, and over all the force, miraculous power, ability, violence and might of the enemy; and nothing shall by any means hurt you."*

Proverbs 31 talks about a virtuous woman: *Virtuous* is translated, (*Chayil*: a force, whether of men, means or other resources; an army, wealth, virtue, valor, strength, might, power, riches, strength, strong, substance, train, valiantly, valour, virtuously, war, worthy.)[3]

This is not some weak, pitiful, beat down, powerless little thing, but this woman of God has learned that she is to be strong in the Lord and in the power of His might. Her strength is in the spirit realm, not laying folks out, not seducing or manipulating people, or doing things to get their attention and favor.

The Bible says in Ephesians 6:10: *"Finally, my brethren, be strong, empowered, increase in strength in the Lord, and in the power or strength of his might."*

She operates in the Spirit realm. She applies pressure in the spirit realm by prayer, faith and the Word of God in her mouth.

The Bible says in Matthew 18:18: *"Verily I say unto you, whatsoever ye shall bind on earth shall be bound in heaven: and whatsoever ye shall loose on earth shall be loosed in heaven."*

Again, Christians are the only people on the planet that can impact the spirit realm in a positive way.

The Bible says in Ephesians 3:20: *"Now unto him that is able to do exceeding abundantly above all that we ask or think, **according to the power that worketh in us.**"*

The Lord wants us to mature spiritually so He can trust us with power, so we can represent Him on the earth.

An example is if you raise a child, but at age thirty he is still functioning as a child, you can't turn over the wealth or your business to him even though he is in line to inherit it. The Lord has some wealth, power and blessings He wants to share with you. Can He trust you? If we are faithful with little he will make us ruler over much.

The Bible says in James 5:15, 16: *"The fervent prayer of the righteous man availeth much"* – avail means it exercises force, makes you able, gives you might, and gives you strength.

See yourself strong in the spirit. I got this example from Pastor Gary Whetstone. "If a policewoman directing traffic raises her hand to stop a large truck that truck will stop. It weighs tons and could easily run her over. However, the driver

will screech to a stop because her uniform represents the whole police force. When little ole you holds your spiritual hand up and says stop to the devil, he doesn't flee because you are bigger or stronger than him or your voice is so loud it frightens him. He flees because standing behind you is big brother Jesus with all power in heaven and in earth saying, 'Make my day.'

You have power in Jesus.

When you will operate in the influence and power given to you, either you'll operate as a woman of God in the power of the Lord or Satan will trick you to take one of the other roads saying, "what you want is down this road" marked romance, money, fame, material things. At the end of each road is a dead end.

All of these things leave you empty and unfulfilled. You are satisfied for a moment, but it is not enough, it's not what your soul and spirit are hungry for. The power you want is in the spirit realm, the high that you crave is in the presence of God. The love and attention that you crave, it is there.

I think God set us up, because Eve was the one who looked away from God seeking something else. Therefore, we would be the first ones to come back to Him. Women are the ones that crave the supernatural realm, good or evil. That's why the churches are full of women and the witch's covens are full of women. Most of the psychics are women. Men are harder to convince about spiritual things.

Don't waste your time looking down roads that lead to dead ends. The power you want is in the Lord. It is available to you; you don't have to be pretty or smart. God will give you as much as you are willing to pay for.

What is the price? **Obedience.** Make a quality decision to live a life of obedience. Jesus is not just your Savior so you can escape hell. He wants to be your Lord. He wants you to present your body a living sacrifice and to bring every thought to the obedience of Christ.

There will be many times that you will mess up and have to repent for your disobedience. Just ask Him to cleanse you from all sin and all unrighteousness and He will. This is a process that takes time, and you have to cooperate with the process of sanctification. This is when the Lord is taking sin out of you.

Be patient with yourself. Just be honest with the Lord. He will progressively show you things in your life that He is not pleased with. Forsake your sin, lay it aside, and He will do the supernatural part of setting you free. As you are getting free, the Lord wants to use you to help others and set them free.

Choose to use every bit of influence you have to encourage people towards the will of God and snatch them out of the clutches of hell. Loving folk to Jesus, shouting the Word, speaking it gently, nurturing people to Him, praying them to him, counseling and even cooking folk into the Kingdom of God are all ways for you to encourage people to do God's will.

Women, God wants to use you for His glory!

Satan used the first woman to turn all mankind away from God. In the last days, God will use women to turn them back to Him. For in the last days He will pour out His spirit on His handmaidens and your daughters will prophecy.

The devil wants you to think prayer, obedience and speaking the Word of the Lord in faith is not working. **Don't stop.** Sometimes the better it works the more the devil acts up because he knows he's losing ground.

When we don't pray, we complain, we speak death, "Oh this will never change, it will never get right," we cry, we get depressed, eat a quart of ice cream, we talk mess on the phone, we buy a new dress…

We must pray instead of worry; worrying is a waste of time. It gives the enemy access to take those words and fear and start to bring them into being.

You must believe that when you put the Word of God in your mouth and begin to declare what He says, in prayer, in conversation, or to yourself in the mirror; it moves things in the Spirit realm to bring it to pass.

When my children get on my nerves the most, I say to myself, "Lord, I thank you, they are the seed of the righteous, they are being taught of you, you're turning their hearts toward the things of God; you're breaking the bondages off their spirits."

It's natural to get on the phone and tell your girlfriend all that life is not. I'm not saying that you can't share your heart. Share the events, but your conclusion must be: however, God is working in his heart, the Lord is on the scene, His healing power is in operation, He is already releasing the funds, and sending me help.

Say to the person that is talking negative to you, "Yeah I hear you, but I want to believe with you that God is turning your mourning into joy. He is convicting this man, He is raining favor, and He already has a better job lined up for you." This takes practice. You must be vigilant because your flesh will always be negative, the world will always be negative, and some saints will be negative. Limit the amount of time you spend with them. Hang with folk that believe God! Listen to Bible teaching CD's and read books. Put the things God promised you up on your mirror and declare them regularly throughout the day.

If we can get an army of women praying, saying, and praising the Word, the devil will be shaking in his boots.

Get a vision for your children and speak over them what you want.

Those of you who glory in being perfectionists, you're basically critical and impatient with others. Your love should cover a multitude of faults and sins. Love covers folk, not constantly exposing them. Stop criticizing people saying, "This is going to help them get better, it will help jolt them out of the problem." NO! Focus on the positive, and where they are negative, pray and believe God with them that the Lord is helping and changing them. Meanwhile, love and accept folk as they are. They belong to God.

The Lord wants you to use that prayer power to kick the devil out of your house. Choose to operate in the power of the Holy Ghost. Do not operate in deception – we must always be careful of using power in the wrong way.

Make these declarations of faith about yourself.

I am a woman of virtue and integrity who loves the Lord my God with all of my heart, mind and soul. I am a woman of obedience who honors God in every area of my life, submitting to authority with a cooperative loving spirit. I am a woman who speaks the Word, and fills my mouth with His Word. I am a worshiping, praying woman who has God's burden for souls and the world. I am available to pray and intercede whenever the Holy Ghost quickens me. Filled with the Spirit, I am a woman of wisdom and wealth, compassed about with favor, and my children and family are blessed of the Lord. I give of my substance, time, talent and energy for the furtherance of the Kingdom of God. I am strong and healthy and bring my body under subjection. I hear and obey the voice of God, and He blesses everything I put my hands to do.

With power comes responsibility. You must make sure you use it for good and not evil.

Notes:

1. The New Strong's Expanded Exhaustive Concordance of the Bible (Red Letter Edition) Copyright©2001 by Thomas Nelson Publishers. Greek Dictionary of the New Testament. - Page 92
2. Ibid. (Greek Dictionary of the New Testament – page 73)
3. Ibid. (Greek Dictionary of the New Testament – page 86)

Chapter 7

Using the Power the Wrong Way

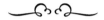

One of the main functions of the "Ezer" is to use her influence to encourage her man towards the will of God for his life. From the very beginning, Eve had a lot of influence over Adam. Influence is power. In order to help him, she would need to be able to influence him.

Adam's mind was blown with this new creature. He said, "bone of my bone, flesh of my flesh, she shall be called woman." He was completely excited. Everything about her completed him. Her body, mind and soul were created just different enough to balance him out, to fulfill and complete him.

You were created to influence; it is in your genes. Everything about Eve was designed to influence Adam. If we do not use this power in a positive, godly way we will use it in a negative way like Eve. Then Satan contaminates our influence, and we will push with a hellish agenda.

There are seven levels of deception that Satan uses through the Christian woman to get her to influence in the negative with his purpose of killing, stealing and destroying. We are tricked into thinking we're doing the right thing but have been subtly deceived. Satan wants to either destroy us or use us, because we were created to influence. Remember our tendency to want to run after him but also run over him. You know we want to run things, and many of us believe we could probably do a better job at running the world.

Therefore, when the enemy contaminates our power, we will use our pretty faces or our nice figure to get male attention and influence them. We show a little cleavage, raise our skirt hems, wear a split that goes all the way up, or wear form-fitting clothes. If we don't have a great body or pretty face we use our mouth.

Some of us have tongues that cut like a sword. We are known by our family and friends for that mouth filled with death, criticism, judging, negativity, and complaining. Some will use that tongue to flatter and seduce, others push for power in the world, with careers, positions and titles.

Some of us are convinced that money is the cure all, even if we have to get a sugar daddy. I saw a group of women on television ready to marry a man sight unseen just because he was a millionaire.

Then some women use a combination:

We use beauty to get money.
We use sex to get power.
We use our mouths to get power.
We use our money to get material things.
I'm still talking to Christian women…

Satan is still trying to offer women power. That is what witchcraft is all about. Witches, psychics, spiritual advisors and readers are usually women. Both spiritual kingdoms want to give you power. Satan wants to offer you power, but he knows you're a Christian, so he must be very subtle.

Let's look at the seven levels of deception through which Satan tries to offer false power and ultimately destroy the Christian woman.

Deception 1: God's Will/ My Way

You need to get the whole counsel of God. In our zeal, we get enough truth, and we run off to change the world in our own strength. God told you, "I'm taking you to Broad Street." You didn't wait to hear: when do we leave, are we taking a bus, car or bike? Which streets we will use? If you are a woman who is aggressive by nature, ambitious, a go getter, you're going to have to watch out for this ploy. These characteristics in the natural world can help bring you success, but in the spiritual realm they can be deadly.

The Lord wants us to be totally dependent on Him. If anyone would have the scoop on how God thinks, it would be Jesus. If anyone could assume and run on ahead, it should be Jesus. I imagine He had a heart to want to fix everything more than any of us, but He was totally dependent on the Father; day by day, moment by moment obedience. He tuned in and only did what the Father said.

The Bible says in John 5:19: *"Verily, verily, I say unto you, the Son can do nothing of himself but what he seeth the Father do; for what things soever he doeth these also doeth the son likewise."*

If Jesus has to be totally dependent and obedient, what makes you think you can run ahead and pick the best way to get to Broad St, fulfill the vision or accomplish the dream He has put in you? Our example is Sarai. She heard the promise that Abraham would have a son, so she comes up with her way to get to God's will and sends her concubine in to lay with her husband, and it is the beginning of a feud that has gone on for generations.

<u>2nd level of Deception</u> – God Needs my Help – Now this seems similar to the first, but this is a deeper deception. There is a flaw in how this woman sees God and His ability and power.

These are all very well meaning folk. Rebekah felt like God needed her help, so she came up with this elaborate scheme to make sure her baby, Jacob, got all the goodies of the inheritance because he was her favorite. She heard God say that the elder would serve the younger, but she believed God needed her help.

Rescuers have to be very careful of this level. Level one just ran off without getting complete instructions. Level two feels that she is supposed to pull out the maps and assist God with the plan to go to Broad St. (She has a good sense of direction, and she has talked with others who have been there.) This comes out in her marriage, ministry, parenting etc.

God does not need you! He just wants to include you; He wants you to be a partaker.

The Bible states in Colossians 1:12: *"Giving thanks unto the Father which hath made us meet to be partakers of the inheritance of the saints in light. He knows if you fellowship in the suffering you'll fellowship in the glory."*

Know what God has told you to do—that's it. Know what His responsibility is; take your hands off of God's stuff. You cannot make your husband and children get saved, or act right. You are not the Holy Spirit. It is not your job to convict people and make them feel guilty.

This is one of the keys to mental health. <u>Only do what God tells you to do.</u> You do not have to worry about the results, the outcome or the plan. **Stop rescuing people.** Pain helps them to grow.

You get in trouble when you start operating outside the scope of your responsibility. For example, if you decide to beat someone else's child, that is not your scope. In addition to the trouble you will bring on yourself, it will burn you out.

<u>3rd Level of Deception – I Trust my Spiritual Intuition above the Word of God</u>

"I had a dream; I had a vision, my mama saw in the spirit realm. The voice didn't line up with the Word, but I had cold sweats."

Make sure what you see, hear and feel are judged by the Word of God. Women must stop living by their emotions—nobody cares how you feel.

Like David, you command your soul and your emotions to line up with the Word.

The Bible states in I John 4:1-3: *"Beloved, believe not every spirit, but try the spirits whether they are of God, because many false prophets are gone out into the world."*

There is an increase of the demonic influence in the world. Furthermore, remember, Eve is more susceptible to satanic deception, that's why she needed a spiritual covering.

Satan can give you a dream, a vision. Stay within the parameters of the authority system God has set up. You can have the right word given in the wrong way at the wrong time and bring death.

Submit to your pastor, leaders, and husband. Don't say, *"I don't care what nobody says, I'm gonna preach the Word."* **Wrong** – when you move in rebellion you move in witchcraft.

If God called you, it is His responsibility to work things out, and while He is, He works on your flesh and your character, bringing forth some Fruit of the Spirit. Therefore, when He exalts you in due season you'll be ready. If you believe that He is working all things together for good even if your leader is wrong, folk are on the wrong track or your husband is wrong, you stay in order. God will protect you in the middle of mess, bless you and allow it to work together for your good.

4th Level of Deception – "I am a Mighty Woman of God and Men Are Trying to Hold Me Down"

Don't have an axe to grind with men. Man is not the enemy; we wrestle not against flesh and blood. Be careful of bitterness – you will just minister out of your hurt. Especially, those called to ministry. There are subtle attacks of the enemy, and if you are not careful you will spend your time justifying your right to preach and fall into 'sanctified fussing'. Some believe they must act and look like a man to be heard or valid. Get on your face before the Lord; be strong in the Lord and in the power of His might. No one can deny the anointing; the power of God will make room for you and open doors. You don't have to push them down.

I had to speak from a choir loft at a church that did not believe women should stand in the pulpit. You don't have to call me Pastor, Dr, or Rev; I am just a servant of the King. I can minister from the choir loft or the basement. As long as I please the Lord and the Holy Ghost moves, and God moved! Don't take this stuff personally; Satan wants to stop the gospel, the Word in you. Do you want glory, fame, and honor? Are you ministering so you can feel good about yourself? Are your motives pure for ministry? Challenges and problems will reveal your real motives.

By the way, this anger with men also opens women up to that spirit of lesbianism floating through the church.

5th Level of Deception- Mutiny! Our example is Miriam – Girlfriend didn't want Moses with that black woman. Whenever you are pushing or cooperating with mutinies against authority you better check yourself. *"We don't like the decision the Pastor made and were going to set up a meeting,"* Girl, you better check yourself.

The Bible states in Hebrews 13:17: *"Obey them that have the rule over you and submit yourselves for they watch for your souls as they that must give account, that they may do it with joy and not with grief; for that is unprofitable to you."*

The Bible states in Proverbs 6:16: *"These six things doth the Lord hate: yea seven are an abomination unto him....he that soweth discord among brethren."*

God hates when you sow strife and discord...abomination is a strong word.

Even if the Pastor is wrong or living in sin, it is better for you to leave rather than stay there and fight. The Bible gives you a process to confront authority systems; mutiny is not one of them. "Touch not mine anointed neither do my prophet no harm", is still in the Word. (I Chronicles 16:22). You better back up, I have seen folk die messing with God's leadership.

6th Level – Jezebel – Usually married to Ahab, a weak man. This spirit wants power. It can operate in men or women. This woman may be very influential, thinks she is more spiritual than others, and may have lots of dreams and visions. She rebels against authority. Sometimes she will try to work through her husband or group pressure. Sometimes there is some sexual perversion with this spirit. She will even try to seduce for the purpose of power. She is spiritually deceived. There are different levels of operating in this spirit. Deal with your own rebellion and humble yourself.

7th Level – Religious Witch – This is a mature Jezebel spirit - This woman is in total deception.

I met a woman in the islands who said, *"If I have to use a spirit of Jezebel to get this Pastor out, I will."* She was already married to a pastor that she had taken from another woman. I watched her seduce another young married pastor right before my eyes. She wanted to control and manipulate. Our Biblical example is the woman with the spirit of divination (Acts 16:19. Deal with your own controlling spirit; lay it down, let God control you and your world.

God wants to give you power! Some of it came automatically when you got saved whether you knew it or how to operate it.

The Bible states in John 1:12: *"But as many as received him to them gave he power to become the sons of God..."*

The Bible states in Acts 1:8: *"But ye shall receive power after that the Holy Ghost is come upon you and ye shall be witnesses unto me."*

God is preparing a glorious future for his Bride, the church, and he has called you to a hope, a bright future. "I know the plans I have for you saith the Lord, plans to prosper you, plans never to harm you, plans to give you hope and a future" He is looking for vessels to show himself strong through. He wants to give out power. However, the higher levels of power are reserved for those who walk in obedience. The more obedient you are, you the more power you will walk in.

Women, you are called, destined, and ordained to walk in the power of God. How do you make sure you do not get deceived and used by the enemy? Most of the women who end up operating in deception started out as well-meaning, even having a zeal to serve God.

The only way we can avoid self-deception is self-examination.

Make these declarations of faith about yourself.

Lord, I thank you for the blood of Jesus that cleanses from all sin. Please forgive me for any areas of disobedience in my life, and any degree of rebellion. Please separate me from all who have ungodly, deceptive motives. I thank you that you are breaking all ungodly soul ties. Please forgive me for being controlling in anyway. I acknowledge you as Lord and Master of my life. You have all wisdom and understanding and I renounce the works of the enemy in my life. I plead the blood of Jesus over my mind, spirit and soul. You, Lord, are my strength, wisdom and protection.

Please expose the lies of the enemy so that I may walk in your truth in all my ways. Please fill me with your Holy Spirit. By faith I put on the whole armor of God.
In Jesus' Name,

Amen

Chapter 8

Let a Woman Examine Herself

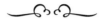

God will not bless a woman with power whom He cannot trust. You cannot be trusted if you are not honest with yourself and with God. When you are honest, you will confess your sins, and you will yield to the chastening of the Lord. You will know when you are sick and seek healing from God. Through this honesty you will stay spiritually healthy. **Power in unhealthy hands can corrupt and destroy others and yourself.**

We are told by God to examine ourselves, judge ourselves, and know ourselves. Unfortunately, our culture is not geared to self-examination. We are very materialistic, comfort oriented, and we are not deep thinkers. In fact, we use many things to drown out quiet thought: blasting T.V, radios, surround sound music, theaters, loud concerts, amusement parks, even music in the elevator. We have a party mentality in this country. There is little encouragement to take quiet walks or sit and meditate on the Word. We have raised a whole generation on T.V, and they learned their ABC's on Sesame Street with folk jumping and singing each letter. We judge ourselves by others. We dress and talk according to what the media tells us is cool. We all want to be one of the beautiful people. We live in a high-paced, stressful, competitive, angry world. Our nation is throwing off all restraints and even our children are killing without remorse.

Satan does not want you to get still. He does not want you to be aware of yourself nor does he want you to hear God.

The Bible states in Numbers 9:8: "And Moses said unto them, *Stand still, and I will hear what the LORD will command concerning you.*"

The Bible states in Joshua 3:8: *"And thou shalt command the priests that bear the Ark of the Covenant, saying, When ye are come to the brink of the water of Jordan, **ye shall stand still in Jordan**. And Joshua said unto the children of Israel, **Come hither, and hear the words of the LORD your God.**"*

The Bible states in I Samuel 9:27: *"And as they were going down to the end of the city, Samuel said to Saul, Bid the servant pass on before us, (and he passed on,) but **stand thou still a while, that I may show thee the word of God.**"*

The Bible states in I Kings 19:12: *"And after the earthquake a fire; but the LORD was not in the fire: and after the fire **a still small voice.**"*

The Bible states in II Chronicles 20:17: *"Ye shall not need to fight in this battle: set yourselves, **stand ye still, and see the salvation of the LORD** with you, O Judah and Jerusalem: fear not, nor be dismayed; tomorrow go out against them: for the LORD will be with you."*

The Bible states in Exodus 14:13: *"And Moses said unto the people, Fear ye not, **stand still, and see the salvation of the LORD,** which he will show to you today: for the Egyptians whom ye have seen today, ye shall see them again no more forever."*

Even the saints can rip and run and do so much that they rarely find time to sit quietly in the presence of the Lord. We can use Christian busy work to distract us from the still small voice of God. Christian busy work is anything you are doing that takes you out of the will of God. There are many good things you can do, but what does God want you to do?

Jesus could have been healing people twenty-four hours a day; He could have set up a "feed the hungry ministry" after he fed the 5,000; He could have walked through all the burial grounds and raised folk from the dead twenty-four hours a day after His success with Lazarus. He could have decided not to die but just spend his time casting out demons. No, He said, "I do what the Father says do."

You won't know what the Father wants unless you get still. Jesus constantly was going off alone to be with the Father. Some of us don't want to be alone, we are afraid to be alone. We don't want to be alone with God or ourselves. Distractions keep us from being self-aware and God aware.

Three things can happen when you get still:

1. You can hear God.
2. You can perceive the spiritual realm.
3. You can examine and be aware of yourself.

Part of spiritual maturity is to have well-trained senses. Just like you have five senses to perceive the natural realm, you have spiritual senses to perceive the spiritual realm.

The Bible states in Hebrews 5:13: *"For every one that useth milk is unskilful in the Word of righteousness: for he is a babe. 14 But strong meat belongeth to them that are of full age, **even those who by reason of use have their senses exercised to discern both good and evil.**"*

As you tune in, not only will you become more aware of the spirit realm, you will also hear God. This is also the best time to examine and be aware of yourself. It is very important that we judge ourselves.

The Bible states in I Corinthians 11:28-32 (NLT): *"That is why you should examine yourself before eating the bread and drinking from the cup. For if you eat the bread or drink the cup unworthily, not honoring the body of Christ, you are eating and drinking God's judgment upon yourself. That is why many of you are weak and sick and some have even died. But if we examine ourselves, we will not be examined by God and judged in this way. But when we are judged and disciplined by the Lord, we will not be condemned with the world."*

I looked up the word 'judge' each time it is used in these verses, and there were several different meanings. So even though different words were translated to be 'judge', the original Greek words had slightly different meanings. Knowing the original translation of a few of the other key words clarifies this verse even farther. This is how it reads:

But let a man <u>examine</u> (test, approve, discern)) [1] *himself and so let him eat of that bread and drink of that cup. For he that eateth and drinketh unworthily, eateth and drinketh damnation to himself, not discerning, the Lord's body. For this cause many are <u>weak</u> (feeble, diseased, impotent,)* [2] *among you, and many <u>sleep</u> (dead)* [3] *. For if we would, <u>judge</u> ourselves (separate thoroughly, withdraw from, oppose, discriminate, hesitate, and contend)* [4] *we should not be <u>judged</u> (tried, condemned, punished, avenged, damned, sued, called in question, sentenced)* [5] *by God. But when we are judged we will not be <u>judged</u> (against, sentence, damn, condemned)* [6] *with the world.*

The New Revised Standard Version translates it like this:

I Corinthians 11: 28 Examine yourselves, and only then eat of the bread and drink of the cup. [29] For all who eat and drink without discerning the body eat and drink judgment against themselves. [30] For this reason many of you are weak and ill, and some have died. But if we judged ourselves, we would not be judged. [32] But when we are judged by the Lord, we are disciplined so that we may not be condemned along with the world.

Choices:

1. Judge yourself
2. Let God judge and discipline you
3. Or stay with the world and let God sentence and condemn you.

You will not have time to judge others. It will take all your time to get yourself in order. Judge yourself—this is from the Hebrew word *diakrino*; **to separate thoroughly**, i.e. to withdraw from, or oppose; to discriminate [7], to separate thoroughly, there are four things you must separate and know:

1. Your actions
2. Your words
3. Your attitudes
4. Your motives

Some of us are aware of our actions but not our attitudes. So when a person tries to tell you that even though you said the right words you had a bad attitude, you don't have a clue that you have an attitude problem. Then some people have all the right actions and words but the wrong motives. Other folk mean well but they consistently do and say the wrong things.

Separating and being aware of yourself on all levels is going to take all your time and attention. You will not have time to judge anyone else. We are very complex. You have to check your spirit, check your thoughts, check your attitude, check your words, and check your motives.

The Word of God helps us with this.

The Bible states in Hebrews 4:12-13 (Amp): *"For the Word of God is full of living power. It is sharper than the sharpest knife, cutting deep into our innermost thoughts and desires. It exposes us for what we really are. Nothing in all creation can hide from him. Everything is naked and exposed before his eyes. This is the God to whom we must explain all that we have done.*

KJV says it divides asunder of soul and spirit, and of the joints and marrow, and is a discerner of the thoughts and intents of the heart.

The Word of God is quick, lively, powerful, active, effectual and sharp. It helps us to separate the soul and spirit, our body's needs, our thoughts, and even the motives of our hearts.

Be aware of your temperament weaknesses and ministry gift weaknesses. You should learn about all these differences and the weaknesses that come with them. Don't rationalize your weaknesses but yield that temper, yield that critical tongue, and give up that laziness. Go through the process that God has to deliver you.

The Bible states in **Romans 14:10-13:** *"So why do you condemn another Christian? Why do you look down on another Christian? Remember, each of us will stand personally before the judgment seat of God. For the Scriptures say, "'as surely as I live,' says the Lord, 'every knee will bow to me and every tongue will confess allegiance to God.'" Yes, each of us will have to give a personal account to God. So don't condemn each other anymore. Decide instead to live in such a way that you will not put an obstacle in another Christian's path."* (NLT)

The Bible states in Psalms 26:1: *"Judge me, O LORD."* 'Judge' here translates from the Hebrew, it means to investigate, examine, prove, tempt. [8]

The Bible states in II Corinthians 13:5: *"Examine yourselves to see if your faith is really genuine. Test yourselves. If you cannot tell that Jesus Christ is among you, it means you have failed the test."* (NLT)

The Bible states in Matthew 7:1-5: *"Stop judging others and you will not be judged. For others will treat you as you treat them. Whatever measure you use in judging others, it will be used to measure how you are judged. And why worry about a speck in your friend's eye when you have a log in your own? How can you think of saying, 'Friend, let me help you get rid of that speck in your eye,' when you can't see past the log in your own eye? Hypocrite! First get rid of the log from your own eye; then perhaps you will see well enough to deal with the speck in your friend's eye..."* (NLT)

The Bible states in I Corinthians 4:5: *"So be careful not to jump to conclusions before the Lord returns as to whether or not someone is faithful. When the Lord comes, he will bring our deepest secrets to light and will reveal our private motives. And then God will give to everyone whatever praise is due. "Stop judging others and you will not be judged. Stop criticizing others, or it will all come back on you. If you forgive others, you will be forgiven."* (NLT)

This even applies to your husband. You are not called to give an account for him. This excuse will not work with God, "Well, I couldn't do what you told me because he didn't do what he was supposed to do."

Know yourself and your issues. Accept yourself, accept your strengths and your weaknesses; then ask and cooperate with the Lord to heal you. **Know your touchy spots.** If you grew up with someone telling you that you were stupid, it wounded your self-image. Thirty years later if someone even implies that you are stupid, you go off, get hostile, all this anger from your childhood gets pulled up, and your response is completely out of proportion. The rest of us look at you like you are crazy.

Know your buttons. Confess your faults one to another. Be real with yourself and others. Be patient with yourself. Cooperate with God's process to fix you.

You are not in competition with anyone else. The purpose for knowing and being real about your weaknesses is so you can allow God to heal you. Don't walk around bragging about speaking your mind because you are a prophet. Let God change you. Cooperate with His process to crucify your mess. Ask the Lord like David to set a watch over your tongue. Think and pray before you speak.

<u>Judgment Seat</u>

We spend 90% of our time and energy living to make sure we are comfortable for a brief moment in comparison to eternity. We are not judged for our sins at the Judgment seat of Christ. When you confess them, they are under the blood. However, we will all be judged for what we have done for the Lord and our motives for that service.

The Bible says in I Corinthians 4:4-5: *"My conscience is clear, but that isn't what matters. It is the Lord himself who will examine me and decide. So be careful not to jump to conclusions before the Lord returns as to whether or not someone is faithful. When the Lord comes, he will bring our deepest secrets to light and will reveal our private motives. And then God will give to everyone whatever praise is due."* (NLT)

The Bible says in I Corinthians 3:11-14: *"For other foundation can no man lay than that is laid, which is Jesus Christ. Now if any man builds upon this foundation gold, silver, precious stones, wood, hay, stubble;* **Every man's work shall be made manifest:** *for the* *day shall declare it, because it shall be revealed by fire; and the* **fire shall try every man's work of what sort it is.** *If any man's work abide which he hath built thereupon, he shall receive a reward. If any man's work shall be burned, he shall suffer loss: but he himself shall be saved; yet so as by fire."*

The Bible says in I Corinthians 3:11-15 (NLT): *"But there is going to come a time of testing at the judgment day to see what kind of work each builder has done. Everyone's work will be put through the fire to see whether or not it keeps its value. If the work survives the fire, that builder will receive a reward. But if the work is burned up, the builder will suffer great loss. The builders themselves will be saved, but like someone escaping through a wall of flames."*

The Bible says in II Corinthians 5:8-11: *"Yes, we are fully confident, and we would rather be away from these bodies, for then we will be at home with the Lord. So our aim is to please him always, whether we are here in this body or away from this body. For we must all stand before Christ to be judged. We will each receive whatever we deserve for the good or evil we have done in our bodies. It is because we know this solemn fear of the Lord that we work so hard to persuade others. God knows we are sincere, and I hope you know this, too."* (NLT)

You will not be standing before an old man in a rocking chair, or a little lamb in a cradle. He has **all** power in heaven and in earth! Your soul is eternal. You get to determine the quality of your life for eternity during this brief amount of time you have on this planet. Don't focus all your attention on trying to live the good life now and forget you have an eternity to prepare for. Your life here is just a vapor, a moment compared to your eternity. It seems like it is a long time (50 years or 60 years if you get that long), but it is just a moment compared to eternity.

The Bible says in Daniel 12:2: *"Many of those whose bodies lie dead and buried will rise up, some to everlasting life and some to shame and everlasting contempt. Those who are wise will shine as bright as the sky, and those who turn many to righteousness will shine like stars forever."* (NLT)

Yield your life to God and see everything that you do as worship to Him and for His glory. (Whether ye eat, drink, or whatever you do, do all for the glory of God.)

Glorify Him on your job, by not going to work late and thus stealing time from your job. Glorify Him in your relationships by submitting to your husband, and obeying your pastor as unto the Lord. Glorify Him in ministry, serve in church as you sing on the choir, visit the sick, preach, and pray as unto the Lord, work in the community, and turn people to righteousness, and you will *shine like stars forever*.

People are important to God. You help people, love people, care for and nurture people, protect, pray for, teach and guide people. This is what makes God happy. He doesn't care about you being a great evangelist, getting your book published, preaching before thousands, getting a record deal, or getting your doctorate; God cares about **how you treat His people**.

Judge yourself—you will stand before God, all the angels will be there, all the saints that ever lived will be there.

You've heard the song, only what you do for Christ will last. This does not mean that you have to quit your job, but you give your life to the Lord. Everything you do, you do all for the glory of God. Your whole life becomes an expression of worship for God.

Make sure that what you do is for the right reasons, and the right motives. Here is a good check: If you do some service for the Lord and your pastor does not mention you, or you don't get the saint of the month award, they wouldn't let you sing your song, read your poem, or preach your sermon and you get irritated, hurt, and mad—your motives were wrong.

We do things for all kinds of reasons. If it's for being seen, being heard, getting approval, getting even, getting attention, for fame, money, or power, God's purifying fire will burn it up. This is why you don't have time to worry about somebody else. If they were wrong, everyone will know in the end.

Do you want to stand before God with nothing and say, "I was busy, I had to finish my degree, I wanted to have a nice job, I wanted a new car, a nice house, I didn't have time to serve you, Lord." You gave me your life, but I wanted the good life that takes time and energy, money and focus. I did go to church periodically and gave to the Red Cross."

God wants you to have the good life. He gives you the formula – "seek ye first the kingdom of God and its righteousness and He will add all these things unto you." Pick up your cross and die daily to what you want and He will give it to you. Or you can spend your whole life trying to have the good life, put God on hold and just run to church when you feel like it or when you have a problem. You're too busy to serve Him. You will have nothing to show for your life in eternity.

The Bible states in I Corinthians 3:15: *"But if the work is burned up, the builder will suffer great loss. The builders themselves will be saved, but like someone escaping through a wall of flames." (NLT)*

I challenge you to put the Lord in the center of your life, it's scary to die to your dreams and your wants, and turn your life, your business, your career, your marriage, and your children over to God. However, He really is smarter than you and me. Stop trying to set up your little plans, lay it all down and say to God "whatever you want me to do."

Most of us have said to the Lord, "I want to serve you with my life," but we try to make God a consultant for our plans. God does not want to consult you on your plan. Nail it to the cross; let your dreams, plans, and expectations die. Turn it over to God.

The Bible states in Proverbs 16:3 (Amp):

"You will want what he wants for you, delight in him, he will give you the desires of your heart. He wants to give you power, authority, honor, but he calls the shots, he is the director, producer, give him obedience and love. He will bless you far above what you could ever dream."

The Bible states in Galatians 2:19-20: *"For when I tried to keep the law, I realized I could never earn God's approval. So I died to the law so that I might live for God. I have been crucified with Christ. I myself no longer live, but Christ lives in me. So I live my life in this earthly body by trusting in the Son of God, who loved me and gave himself for me."* (NLT)

Examine yourself, my sister. Make sure you are not trapped with the same trap as our mother, Eve…rebellion.

Make these declarations of faith about yourself.

Lord, I thank you for your faithfulness to Your Word. Your promises are true. If there be any wicked way in me, create in me a clean heart and renew a right spirit within me. I lay aside every weight and sin that would turn me from You. I choose to press toward the mark of the prize of the high calling of God in Christ Jesus. Thank you for being my righteousness, and I stand complete in You.

Notes:

1. The New Strong's Expanded Exhaustive Concordance of the Bible (Red Letter Edition) Copyright©2001 by Thomas Nelson Publishers. Greek Dictionary of the New Testament. Page 71
2. Ibid. (Greek Dictionary – page 44)
3. Ibid. (Greek Dictionary – page 141)
4. Ibid. (Greek Dictionary – page 66)
5. Ibid. (Greek Dictionary – page 145)
6. Ibid. (Greek Dictionary –page 145)
7. Ibid. (Greek Dictionary of the New Testament – page 73)
8. The New Strong's Expanded Exhaustive Concordance of the Bible (Red Letter Edition) Copyrigh©2001 by Thomas Nelson Publishers. The Hebrew and Aramaic Dictionary. Page 288)

Chapter 9

Am I a Rebellious Woman?

One of the main things we must watch out for as women is rebellion. It will drain your spiritual strength very quickly and make you a candidate for demonic deception. However, learning how to live under authority propels you to new levels of promotion.

The Bible states in I Peter 2:21-23: *"This suffering is all part of what God has called you to. Christ, who suffered for you, is your example. Follow in his steps. He never sinned, and he never deceived anyone. He did not retaliate when he was insulted. When he suffered, he did not threaten to get even. He left his case in the hands of God, who always judges fairly." (NLT)*

The Bible states in I Peter 3:1: *"In the same way, you wives must accept the authority of your husbands, even those who refuse to accept the Good News. Your godly lives will speak to them better than any words. They will be won over by watching your pure, godly behavior."* (NLT)

There is a correlation between suffering, submission and spiritual victory. God's laws are opposite to the world. In the kingdom of God, the quickest way up is down. All of the saints are told to submit:

Paul asks the Corinthians to yield to good leadership in I Corinthians 16:16. Ephesians 5:21 tells us to submit one to another. In James 4:7, we are told to submit to God. I Peter 2:13 says to submit to every ordinance of the law and authorities.

I Peter 5:5 says younger ministers should submit to the elder.

However, there is special emphasis put on women submitting, especially wives, and this submission is characterized as suffering. All Christians are called to suffer. Christ was our example. Follow in His steps.

The Bible states in I Peter 2:23: *"He did not retaliate when he was insulted. When he suffered, he did not threaten to get even. He left his case in the hands of God, who always judges fairly."* (NLT)

But then a special connection is made to women, *"In the same way wives submit…"* I believe the Lord emphasizes submission to women because it was through Eve that Satan was able to bring destruction.

Living under Order

The enemy has used women from the very first woman and throughout history, to rebel against authority. Let me give you some motivation:

God's response to rebellion is in James chapter four verse six. God sets himself against the proud, but he shows favor to the humble. He resists the proud. *Resists* means to [1] range oneself against, i.e. oppose. The root Greek word for resist is [2] *Tasso*, which means: to arrange in an orderly manner, i.e. assign or dispose (to a certain position or lot) appoint, determine, ordain, and set.

The word for submit is [3] *hupotasso*, to subordinate, to obey, be under obedience, put under, subdue unto, make subject to. It is a military term.

Either you *hupotasso* yourself or God will *tasso* you. Either you subject yourself and put yourself under obedience or God will resist you by arranging or assigning you a certain position. Those who do not submit because of a root of pride, God will humble.

The Bible states in I Samuel 15:23: *"For rebellion is as the sin of witchcraft, and stubbornness is as iniquity and idolatry."*

Rebellion opens your life to demonic invasion.

Be sober; be vigilant because your adversary the devil as a roaring lion walketh about seeking whom he may devour. For any victory in war there must be order, a hierarchy of authority, and obedience to orders. The difference in a riot and a battle is order. I saw a movie where the peasants were revolting against an evil king. The king's soldiers had horses and weapons but the peasants only had farming tools. There was loose leadership and disorder among the peasants. They lost badly. A few years later, they chose to get under the leadership of a military leader. He trained them, organized them, and they moved in obedience and order and even with just farming tools they beat the king's army.

You cannot do spiritual warfare to protect yourself, your home and family or have victory in your church **if you are not under order.** There is a set arrangement by God, an assignment, a certain position, and you must choose to get under and follow that arrangement. As unto the Lord you choose to submit to the authority systems God puts in your life. This is a military term. It doesn't have anything to do with want you want to do.

Submission in the family, the church and the Body of Christ has to do with survival, overcoming, and winning the war. If you are out of order, your enemy will kill you. Most of us do not think of ourselves as rebellious, so I want to give you some manifestations of rebellion, and then I want us to talk about some areas of rebellion you see in your life. Remember, the root is pride:

1. **Deuteronomy 31:27 talks about rebellion and having a stiff neck.** It includes the following: being severe, churlish, cruel, grievous, hardhearted, impudent, obstinate, rough, sorrowful, stiff-necked, and stubborn.
2. **Jonah rebellion –quiet, non-confrontative.** Jonah did not fuss or complain to God, he just went the other way. Be very aware of your behavior. You may not ever verbalize the complaint in your mind. Your best indicator is your actions. You can weep and sing "I Surrender All" but if you never obey or fulfill your promise to God, it's just drama.
3. **Cursing, lying, violence, and quarrels are also indications of pride in your life.**

A rebellious heart stirs up strife. If there is always conflict around you, every boss you have, every church you go to, everybody around you is a problem; there might be some pride in you that is stirring up strife.

4. **Passive aggressive behavior**– You can be a very quiet introvert who will verbally comply with authority. "Yeah, sure dear, I'll wash the dishes," the more you say it the higher the mountain of dirty dishes. Passive aggressive behavior is similar to the Jonah rebellion, but it is more on an unconscious level. Many times the person is not always aware of their own level of rebellion. You may be late all the time, or conveniently forgetting what you don't want to do, even getting tired or sick when it comes time to obey the request. These are manifestations of rebellion.

5. **Controlling and manipulating people (a pride problem)**. Manipulating others, even when you are doing it "for their own good," is a form of witchcraft. That's the goal of witchcraft, to control other people's behavior.

6. **Being a rescuer.** The sailors that were traveling with Jonah tried to save him rather than throw him in the sea as he requested. When they rowed harder the storm raged more. As soon as they tossed him overboard, the pressure was off of them, the storm stopped and God could hold Jonah and discipline him until he was ready to obey God. Some of life's consequences break us and bring us to a place of surrender. They are allowed and sometimes orchestrated by God. He definitely chastens and scourges those that He loves like a loving parent. You must trust the fact that God loves that person more than you love that person, and that He is well able to take care of them.

7. **Being critical, judgmental, and impatient.** Pride is always critical and judgmental of others.

Pride brings you low. It leads to your destruction and some type of fall.

What characteristics of pride or rebellion have you seen in your life? If you are honest and examine yourself, it will be more than one; you might have to put a check by all of them. (Been there, done that.)

Identify those characteristics and then begin to humble yourself so that God does not have to prepare a great fish to swallow you up until you yield to God. Do you want God resisting you because of pride? Can He flow in every aspect of your life?

Pride leads to self deception. It opens the door for demonic deception. You become spiritually blind, thinking you're ok. You become very vulnerable to an enemy that you can't see. That is why pride leads to destruction. It feels natural, even powerful, to rebel, but it will destroy you and others that you love. God wants you to have power, but for some very specific reasons. If you are a child of God, you already have the power, oh mighty woman of God. God wants you to change the world! We represent our God on the earth He wants to be strong in us. We are asked to do four things that will be a catalyst for God to use His power in you.

Our part of the partnership with God is to be like the trigger on a gun. When you shoot a gun all you do is pull your finger back, but it starts a chain reaction. You don't actually hit the target, you start the chain reaction. So when God tells you to clap your hands or give the victory shout, or fast or give an offering, some little behavior done in obedience and faith, it is just the trigger. That's why what you do doesn't matter. He can tell you something silly to do, the key is to obey and to do it in faith, and it becomes the trigger for an explosion in the spirit realm (Joshua walking around the walls of Jericho).

When you pull the trigger of faith all kinds of things start moving in the spirit realm. You may get more angelic reinforcements; angels start fighting, binding and gagging demons; they start breaking chains, and demons lose their grip; they start screaming and being tormented; they run. Healing starts falling; things also change in the natural realm. People's attitudes change.

You put tithes in the offering, and it is the trigger that sends angels to start setting up conditions and circumstances that bring you an unexpected check in the mail a week later. You pray for someone on the other side of the city, and the angels go and start cutting ropes of bondage off them, they take the blinders off their eyes and next time you hear from them, you hear that they got saved. What we do in the natural realm in obedience to God triggers a response from God in the Spirit realm that will change our situation.

The Bible states in I Corinthians 3:6, 7: *"I have planted, Apollos watered; but God gave the increase. So then neither is he that planteth any thing, neither he that watereth; but God that giveth the increase."*

We are the trigger on the gun. So the angels sit around waiting for you to pull the trigger; if you don't pray, they don't move. God set it up this way so that we would be involved. He tells you to resist the devil, He tells you whatever you bind on earth, I'll bind in heaven, He tells you put on the whole armour, then He doesn't even say to fight, He just says stand, and stand, and having done all to stand. We are wrestling against spiritual forces. The key in wrestling is to stay on your feet. Jesus already did all the work; he made an open show of the enemy and triumphed over the forces of hell.

I Corinthians 3:9 says we are laborers together with God, we work together with God. He doesn't need us, but He wants us to participate in the struggle so the victory will mean something to us.

Just like you don't actually kill the person with the gun, if you pull the trigger, the law will credit you for killing the person, and you will go to jail. When we pull the spiritual trigger, you don't actually do anything. God and His angels do all the work, but you get credit for it, you get rewards and crowns in glory.

Remember, God wants a wife, a partner, who is involved and ruling with Him. Therefore, what you see wrong with the world, is not God's fault, it's our fault. He made us partners with Him. He gave us authority in the spirit realm and in the natural realm, so we can even just say the word and things move. He gives us authority over Satan and over all His works, He gives us weapons, armour, angels, shields, an army—all at our disposal and then waits for us to pull the trigger.

Most of us don't have a clue. Our priority is what dress we will buy next, making more money, paying our bills, or when we plan to kiss our boyfriend.

He wants to empower you for a purpose. His heart is people. He wants to heal our land, set people free, and break the yokes of bondage. The power is not just so you can get the new car you want; it is so you can be the light of the world and lead people to Him.

Let's look at what we have to do to pull the trigger in I Chronicles 7:14 for God to heal the land. <u>Four things we are told to do:</u>

1. Humble ourselves
2. Pray
3. Seek His Face
4. Turn from our wicked ways

1. **Humble ourselves** – we have covered this in previous chapters
2. **Pray** – to officially intercede, to entreat and make supplications to the judge. Therefore, this is a specific type of prayer for your neighborhood, your city, your nation and the world.

   Your prayer should begin small. Start with your neighborhood. Pray consistently about your neighborhood, cry out to God for mercy and for Him to save people and heal the land. Get a plan, focus, be consistent, and be led of the Lord.

   When I was in college, even though it was a religious institution, there were a lot of young people who were church kids but not saved. The Lord led a friend and me to pray together every day for revival on our campus. We stayed focused for about three months. And then one day the Lord began to move after a meeting as people were just standing around and talking. My husband began witnessing to a young freshman about the Lord. He was a tough corner boy with an earring in his ear. As he listened, a tear began to fall down his cheek, people began singing hymns and a spontaneous move of God just flowed through the group. Many were saved that evening and four or five young men felt the Lord was calling them into the ministry. The move of God started impacting the whole campus. It was awe-inspiring.

   You need to start out with a specific time. It disciplines us to be consistent. The goal is a prayer life. When you are praying all the time and living in the secret place, but that takes a whole reorienting of thought when you focus on the spiritual realm because that's where things start.

3. Seek My Face

You must seek His face, not His hands, not just His blessing. For example, if your kids only asked you for money, you would get a little indignant. It's the same way with God...oh she wants a new job, so now she's praying. She hasn't talked to me all month, but now she's praying.

Obviously, this must be done in spirit and in truth; you can't play any games with God. He knows your real motives and if your heart is turned towards Him, or if you are just running your mouth.

4. Turn from Your wicked ways—When we hear turn from our wicked ways, we think, drinking or drugs. As the people of God, we can't just look at the manifestational sins; we must look at the root sin. Notice the verse does not say sins, but sin. The root sin might be fear but from that root also comes, worry, anxiety and unbelief. We have to be conscious of sins that are of the heart not just behavior: self-righteousness, bitterness, rebellion, back-biting, judging others, racism, jealousy, pride, gluttony, laziness, haughtiness, unforgiveness, and sowing discord.

If I were to ask you to make a list of the top seven worst sins, you might say: murder, rape, stealing, adultery, and the list goes on.

Look at God's list:

The Bible states in Proverbs 6:16-19: *"These six things doth the Lord hate; yea, seven are an abomination unto him; A proud look, a lying tongue, and hands that shed innocent blood. A heart that deviseth wicked imaginations, feet that be swift in running to mischief, a false witness that speaketh lies and he that soweth discord among brethren."*

At least six of those things saints do all the time. Pride, sowing discord... (He said, she said; they don't like you; and we don't have to put up with this mess.)

Pride stirreth up strife. Check yourself. If you had a critical, judgmental parent, you're probably the same way; if you felt rejected, it will be an issue for you; if there is a history of rebellious, mouthy women or irresponsible, abusive men, check yourself. It impacted you in some way, either you will repeat the behavior, or you will go to the other extreme. Both can be a problem.

Are you rude, selfish, self-centered, revengeful, ungrateful, complaining, judgmental, controlling, jealous, or proud? Think about things your enemies have said, sometimes they will tell you the truth that your friends won't. Listen to what your husband keeps saying about you. This is the other reason we learn to speak the truth in love to each other. Sometimes your friends won't know they are mean if you don't tell them in love. Iron sharpeneth iron; we rub up against each other to help polish each other.

We must turn away from the mess in us. Then Satan has no foothold in your life, and then you can take authority and walk in the power of God. You can't party with the devil all night Saturday and then think you can rebuke him on Sunday morning. He will laugh at you. You try to resist, but he won't flee because you didn't do the first part. Submit yourselves therefore unto God. Read this whole passage.

According to the Scriptures in James 4:6-11a: *"But he giveth more grace, wherefore he saith, God resisteth the proud, but giveth grace to the humble. Submit yourselves therefore to God. Resist the devil and he will flee from you. Draw nigh to God, and he will draw nigh to you, cleanse your hands, ye sinners, and purify your hearts, ye double-minded. Be afflicted and mourn and weep; let your laughter be turned to mourning, and your joy to heaviness (repentance) Humble yourselves in the sight of the Lord, and he shall lift you up. Speak not evil one of another brethren."*

The Lord wants to break forth revival and bring deliverance in your neighborhood, your city, this nation and around the world. If we, the people of God, will come out of our bondage, then we can help pull others out of theirs. Furthermore, God can use little old you. The more all of us humble ourselves, seek God, turn from our wicked ways, pray together, and praise the Lord, the more healing we will see. One of my prayers is that pastors around this nation would stop trying to build their own little kingdom and would pray together to take the nation for Jesus. There would be enough souls saved to fill everyone's church.

There is no competition; we are all in the same body, the same army, the same Lord. We are all fighting the same enemy, and it only makes us weak when we are divided. Satan does not even have to waste ammunition on us; he sits back and lets us destroy ourselves. If you purpose to have a lifestyle of humility and prayer, to seek the face of the Lord and lay down everything not like God, He will allow you to walk in His power. Jesus was manifested to destroy the works of the devil. The purpose of your spiritual power is to participate in destroying the works of the devil. You need to be free first, and then you can work to free your family and those whom the Lord sends you to minister to. You cannot be victorious over the enemy of your soul unless you **"stay under order."**

Believe God as you declare His Word:

Lord, I thank You that You have given me power over the enemy and none of his strategies will work against me. Every weapon formed against me is being canceled and made useless. I submit and humble myself unto You, I acknowledge You as Lord of my life. So as I resist the devil he will flee from me. I cast off the spirit of rebellion; I have a teachable and obedient spirit. Lord, I submit to the authority systems that You have set over me, and I commit my way to You.

Notes:

1. The New Strong's Expanded Exhaustive Concordance of the Bible (Red Letter Edition) Copyright©2001 by Thomas Nelson Publishers. Greek Dictionary of the New Testament. - Page 30
2. Ibid. (Greek Dictionary of the New Testament -page 260)
3. Ibid. (Greek Dictionary – page 258 &260)

Chapter 10

Stay Under Order so You Can Fight to Win

S ubmission to authority is one of the foundational principles that you must understand to properly function in the army of the Lord. The spiritual war that we are in is deadlier and much more expansive than any war that man has ever fought in history. We see the destruction of lives in our communities, our men and youth, the drugs and violence. The attack is on the souls of men. The goal is to send them to an eternal hell which is much more devastating than losing your physical life.

The Bible states in Matthew 10:28: *"And do not be afraid of those who kill the body but cannot kill the soul, but rather be afraid of him who can destroy both soul and body in hell"* (Amplified).

Our God reigns, He makes all decisions about eternity.

The Spiritual war that we are in has been going on for generations—the war between good and evil. God created the scenario—He made the angels and He made man. He created the spiritual realm and the natural realm. He created the rules to govern both. He made Lucifer. He saw the stuff in his heart. He made Adam and Eve. He gave each of them their characteristics and tendencies. He knew what was going to happen. This was not some big divine oops where God was taken by surprise. We know this because He set things up and made provision for salvation, even before He created the world.

Revelation 13:8 tells us that Jesus was the lamb that was slain from the foundation of the world.

According to the Scriptures in Ephesians 1:4: *"Even as [in His love] He chose us [actually picked us out for Himself as His own] in Christ before the foundation of the world, that we should be holy (consecrated and set apart for Him) and blameless in His sight, even above reproach, before Him in love."* (Amplified)

The whole plan was made before the world was created. He reigns. He set up the rules and systems for the natural and the spiritual realm. He set up the flow chart. He set up the roles and who would play which part. We really do give the devil too much credit. He is just one of the actors in this production. God even boxed himself in by his own rules. Things like *Hebrews 9:22b: "without the shedding of blood there is no remission of sin."*

Sin cannot be wiped out unless blood is shed. He could have set up a different plan for salvation. He knew when He said it that the blood of bulls and sheep would not satisfy Him but for a moment. It was all a part of His plan. We don't understand the Sovereignty and power of our God. Sometimes we think of Him as an old man in heaven who is just a little stronger than us. No, we are serving the all-powerful, all-knowing, all-wise, ever-present Master of everything. Our little lives are like a lit candle that only has a few years to burn down, and at anytime God can just blow, and you are gone. From His perspective, it is just a few moments, and we are gone. He could do the same to the devil, but He allows him to continue because he serves God's purpose. God sets the boundaries for Satan, determines how far he can go, and what he can do. God does not even get in the fight with Satan. He could destroy Satan with a word, He created him. Instead, He sets up the war that we must fight. Throughout the Word is reference to the war that we are called to fight:

- Whatever you bind on earth, I'll bind in heaven. Whatever you loose on earth, I'll loose in heaven.
- You pray; you stand; you put on the whole armor.

- You have angels; they hearken to the Word that comes out of <u>your</u> mouth.
- Behold I give <u>you</u> power over all the power of the enemy.

Unless we move, He doesn't move.

<u>Why</u>...there is something about the fight and the struggle that is going to bring the best out of us and the best to the top. The cream will rise.

The best folk are going to rise to the top out of the fight. The struggle works the sin out of us. The Bible says in I Peter 4:1: *"...for he that hath suffered in the flesh hath ceased from sin."*

In every army you have privates, those at the bottom, and five-star generals, those at the top. Everybody starts at the bottom, but those that are obedient, submissive to authority, diligent, and faithful, are the ones that rise through the ranks. There is something about the struggle and the warfare that will show what is in you. As they say, the cream will rise to the top.

- Why did Jesus come? Just to make you feel good and bless you and give you a new car, and then take you away to heaven? No!

The Bible states in I John 3:8: *"For this purpose the Son of God was manifested, that He might destroy the works of the devil."*

Remember what God is after. Jesus was the firstborn. He wants many sons and daughters, who will look like Him, represent Him, speak for Him, and love others for Him. He wants sons and daughters who will destroy the works of the devil. He wants to be able to point to you and say look at my child wielding the sword of the Word, taking authority, setting people free, casting out demons, rescuing those in bondage, and doing miracles.

His agenda is different from ours. We want to chill, have comfort, lay on the beach, live well, and all those are fringe benefits of being His children, but He wants an army of sons and daughters who continue to destroy the works of the devil and who can rule with Him.

He gives power to those who know how to submit to authority. The rebellious, the fearful, the lazy, and the disobedient will stay at the bottom of the ranks as buck privates.

You can give yourself whatever title you want, but power comes from God. This is why even now they are reporting more miracles in other nations because they have a greater respect for authority. I heard an interview of the pastor of a church in Africa where the children were laying hands on people, and they were being healed. When their pastor was asked why, he said that Christians have a greater respect for authority in his country than we do in America— we are all about democracy, and having our rights.

That is why many times when the Lord tells us to submit, He also says, "As unto the Lord." That means the measure of your submission to God is how submissive you are to the authority systems God sets up.

- Wives, we can measure how submissive we are to God by how submissive we are to our husbands.
- Children, you can measure how submissive you are to God by how submissive you are to your parents.
- Church members, we can measure how submissive we are to God by how submissive we are to our pastors.
- As pastors we can tell how submissive you are to God by how you submit to the leaders that we put over you. Some people will say they will submit to the pastor, but they refuse to submit to the leader over that ministry. "I'll listen to you, pastor, but I don't respect them."
- That means you are not ready to be in authority over anyone. Wise leaders do not determine who will be leaders by how talented they are, how many degrees they have, how skillful in the Word they are or even how anointed they are, because all of that must come under authority.

It really doesn't have anything to do with the person and whether or not you think they are a good boss, pastor, leader, husband, or governor. I submit because God set up the system. He set up the order and therefore He honors that order and sends down the flow of the anointing, direction and instruction through that system. The system is not based on the people, it is based on God. He watches over to perform it. That is why those that operate under authority get to operate with authority. When God knows you can be under authority, He will make you to operate with His power and authority. God will put you in trying situations to see if you will submit or rebel.

Only those who trust God can submit - The whole system is based upon how much you trust God. God never asks you to trust people; He never tells you they will be fair, or that they will do the right things. The principle of authority doesn't have anything to do with people. It is between you and God and how much you trust Him. He wants you to commit yourself to Him just like Jesus did. He submitted Himself to the death of the cross.

The Bible says in I Peter 2:22-23: *"Who did no sin, neither was guile found in his mouth: Who, when he was reviled, reviled not again; when he suffered, he threatened not; but committed himself to him that judgeth righteously."*

You will never have a position of authority given by God until you begin to learn how to operate under the principle of authority. You are in the fight, whether you like it or not. You were born in the fight – born in sin – you were on the devil's side – he whipped up on you day and night and you had no way to fight back. Now we are on the Lord's side, and He's looking for the cream. I don't know about you, but I want to be the cream that rises to the top.

A woman who wants power but is not satisfied will use her natural powers in negative, manipulative ways. Being satisfied and content is important for a woman to flow in a Godly way. As you humble yourself the Lord will exalt you in due season. When you are exalted, you need to know how to deal with men as a woman in leadership.

Prayer of Consecration:

Lord I yield my life to you, I was bought with a price and I belong to you. I present my body a living sacrifice, wholly and acceptable unto you. Even as I am faithful over a little you will make me ruler over much. I honor the authority systems that you have set up in my life. I commit myself to you. I do not even have to fight my battles, vengeance belongs to you. Thank you that no weapon formed against me will prosper. I am more than a conqueror and since You are for me, no one else can succeed against me. I break ever demonic assignment against my life. I am blessed, prosperous, and victorious. You satisfy me and I will dwell in your presence.

In Jesus Name Amen

Chapter 11

Guidelines for Women in Leadership

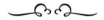

I n most churches there are an abundance of women in leadership, and we thank the Lord for them stepping up to the plate. But, ladies, I know you also want to see strong male leadership. I believe there is enough room for both.

However, if you are a woman in leadership, you must understand the needs and differences of women and men for this to be successful.

Guidelines:

1. Ladies, even though you may be in a position over a man it is necessary that you understand that most men will have an issue with this on a deep level. God created man to be the head in the family. Our society is very male oriented. However, in Christ, there is neither male nor female and in the spirit realm you can soar to whatever height you are willing to pay the price for. There are women in scripture that are definitely in roles of leadership.

2. Because of this there will always be the mixed feelings of "I know you're qualified to do the job, but I'm not happy with it, that's not the way it should be." It is your task to carry yourself with such loving dignity and wisdom that all men around you will be won.

3. Be aware of the need they have to be in charge.
4. Be respectful at all times. Never yell, raise your voice or lose control. Wait until you are calm to talk with them.
5. Speaking the truth in love is a Biblical principle – if you can't say it in love you're not ready to talk about it.
6. Never correct, belittle, or criticize a man in public; pull him to the side. If he feels humiliated it will awaken the warrior in him. Once he gets offended with you remember the Scripture says, "A brother offended is harder to be won than the bars of a castle."
7. When you have to correct someone use a compliment sandwich: begin with the positive, give the correction spoken in love and end with the positive.
8. Correction is done best on the foundation of relationship. Develop a good relationship with the people you are working with. Show concern for them in a general way.
9. Think before you speak. Get information first. The Bible states in Proverbs 18:13: *"He that answereth a matter before he heareth it, it is folly and shame unto him."*

The Bible states in Proverbs 18:7: *"The mouths of fools are their ruin, and their lips a snare to themselves."*

The Bible says in Proverbs 13:3: *"Those who guard their mouths preserve their lives; those who open wide their lips come to ruin."*

10. A soft answer turns away anger. Proverbs 15:1-2: *"A soft answer turns away wrath, but a harsh word stirs up anger. The tongue of the wise dispenses knowledge but the mouths of fools pour out folly."*
11. Learn how to be firm without fussing. Writing things down and then reading from your notes will help you to think about what you want to say before it is communicated and takes the emotions out of it.
12. Let Biblical principles, wisdom and good leadership sense guide you, not your emotions. Being the "emotional, out of control woman" will quickly lose you respect. Think, pray,

seek counsel and bring your feelings under the control of the Holy Spirit.

13. Think about how it will make the other person feel. Take note of their sensitive issues. When you see them flare up in anger, their button has been hit. Ask the Lord to give you wisdom about how to handle them. Take note when the men you deal with get defensive – it will give you a clue to their area of sensitivity.

14. Communicate your respect for the man, even though you have some concerns or issues. Men must feel respected. Focus on his positive traits. Understand the importance of the male ego. It is crucial to dealing with a man, that's what puts the starch in his backbone. If the man has a damaged ego and feels powerless in this society you must use your tongue as a remedy, a medicine to build up what has been torn down. Even if you are over him in authority you still act as a helper by building him up, encouraging his strengths, and speaking the truth in love. You will get a better worker, he will function at his best, and he will support and protect you.

15. You don't have to act like a man to be in leadership. You have powers of influence as a woman. Use them wisely and you will not have to disrespect his manhood. Many men of color are disrespected in our society and in their homes, so they come to church to find their voice and get respect.

16. Submit to the authority over you. Rebelliousness is contagious. If you are rebellious, those under you will rebel.

17. Male/Female dynamics are always present even if the woman is in a place of authority. Sexual issues are also always present. Be aware of how you carry yourself, how you dress, and what you communicate with your clothing. You want to be modest and neat. When you are leading you even need to be a little conservative. Sexy clothing not only distracts men but also makes them less respectful towards you. You want them to look at your face when talking to you and not your cleavage.

18. Use wisdom about physical contact when working closely with someone who is not your husband. It is wise to either have a third party around, meet with the door open, or use the phone or e-mail.

You may ask, "Why do I have to go through all these changes?" This is not a job, most churches and ministries don't have money to motivate people. People have to serve because they want to. Unfortunately, folks don't always do things because of their love for the Lord; they have to be getting something out of it. If the Lord has placed that man under you, you can help and be a blessing to him. Any man that takes his place in our community helps all of us. We need our men to step up to the plate and take the leadership roles to show our sons how to be men. In some Christian circles, women have served for years holding things together.

There is room for both men and women as we learn to submit ourselves one to another. We are different and we lead differently, but God wants to use our maleness and femaleness for His glory.

Being satisfied and content is important for a woman to flow in a Godly way. As you humble yourself the Lord will exalt you in due season. As He exalts you, make sure you learn to be satisfied by Him. A woman of power and position who has not found the joy and fulfillment for her empty places is a dangerous woman.

Make these faith declarations:

Thank You Lord that You are breaking down the walls of partition and men and women, young and old, and every race will worship You and work in unity in the Body of Christ. I thank You for wisdom to lead and minister to your people. I pray that they would see the love of God in me. I am anointed and my gift is making room for me. You fight my battles and make even my enemies to be at peace with me.

Chapter 12

Worshipping Women Are Satisfied, Powerful Women

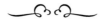

In the last chapter, I listed worship as the fifth step to satisfaction. It is such an important step, not just for satisfaction, but for your growth as a Christian, that I decided to devote a whole chapter to it.

John 4:6-26: *"Now Jacob's well was there. Jesus therefore, being wearied with his journey, sat thus on the well: and it was about the sixth hour. There cometh a woman of Samaria to draw water: Jesus saith unto her, give me to drink. (For his disciples were gone away unto the city to buy meat. Then saith the woman of Samaria unto him, how is it that thou, being a Jew, askest drink of me, which am a woman of Samaria? For the Jews have no dealings with the Samaritans. Jesus answered and said unto her, If thou knewest the gift of God, and who it is that saith to thee, Give me to drink; thou wouldest have asked of him, and he would have given thee living water. The woman saith unto him, Sir, thou hast nothing to draw with, and the well is deep: from whence then hast thou that living water? Art thou greater than our father Jacob, which gave us the well, and drank thereof himself, and his children, and his cattle? Jesus answered and said unto her; Whosoever drinketh of this water shall thirst again: But whosoever drinketh of the water that I shall give him shall never thirst; but the water that I shall give him shall be in him a well of water springing up into everlasting life. The woman saith unto him, Sir, give me this water, that I thirst not, neither come hither to draw. Jesus saith unto her, Go, call thy husband, and come hither. The woman answered and said, I have no husband. Jesus said unto her, Thou hast well said, I have no husband: For thou hast had five husbands; and he whom thou now hast is not thy husband: in that saidst thou truly. The woman saith unto him, Sir, I perceive that thou art a prophet. Our fathers worshipped in this mountain; and ye say, that in Jerusalem is the place where men ought to worship. Jesus saith unto her, Woman, believe me, the hour cometh, when ye shall neither in this mountain, nor yet at Jerusalem, worship the Father. Ye worship ye know not what: we know what we worship: for salvation is of the Jews. But the hour cometh, and now is, when the true worshippers shall worship the Father in spirit and in truth: for the Father seeketh such to worship him. God is a Spirit: and they that worship him must worship him in spirit and in truth. The woman saith unto him, I know that Messias cometh, which is called Christ: when he is come, he will tell us all things. Jesus saith unto her, I that speak unto thee am he."*

It is amazing to me that so many times the Lord Jesus revealed precious nuggets of truth, major principles, and glimpses into the heart of God to women.

John 4: 4 tells us that Jesus needed to go through Samaria. Samaria was the logical way to go to Cana, the shortest, straightest way. The Jews usually went around Samaria because of their disdain and disgust for the Samaritans. The Lord's travel however was based upon who He had to see, heal, or touch, based on instructions from his Father, not the traditions of men.

Do you think there were any coincidences in Jesus' life that He would just happen to go through that area at that moment in time when that particular woman would be there… **No coincidence.**

Jesus is walking miles from Judea to Jacob's well. He had to hear from God exactly when to leave Judea, what pace to walk, what stops to make or not to make. This woman did not go with the other women to the well; she was a woman of bad reputation. She went when nobody else was around. The Bible says Jesus arrived at the well about the sixth hour, which was nine to twelve midday. Jesus got there a little earlier and had time to make sure His disciples went away to get meat. He had to be alone with her because the disciples would obviously have attitudes about this meeting.

There was so much prejudice and separation that the Samaritan woman asked Him, how could you even ask me for a drink. I am a Samaritan woman; the Jews have no dealings with us. Look at verse ten in that passage. Jesus didn't even respond to the bigotry issue, he went to the heart of the spiritual need—"living water."

In verse eleven she goes back to the practical issues, as women are prone to do. Jesus wants to pull you aside to give you life-changing revelation, and you're telling him about the clothes you must wash and the bills you must pay. Because we tend to have to deal with the mundane stuff of life, we sometimes get stuck there. It's a repeat of the Mary/Martha issue. Mary was at the feet of Jesus (Luke 10:38-42) getting a wealth of wisdom from the very mouth of God and Martha is busy dealing with the mechanics of preparing and serving a meal to Jesus and his disciples. It's the first thing that will hinder you from being a woman of worship.

1. Preoccupation with the World

It is our job as the wives, mothers, and the sisters to do all the one thousand things needed to hold together homes and families. God made us to think in a detailed way. The brothers tend to think in a slow, methodical, one direction at a time process. We think quickly and can move from one thing to another. Men see the overall picture, whereas we see the details. Dr. Clarence Walker says this trait makes men more qualified to be the head of the home. "Men see the forest, women see the trees; the head must see the overall forest, while the helpmeet must help him see the tree that he missed."

The level by which your Spirit receives from God has nothing to do with your level of intelligence, how many years of college you have or how deep and philosophical you think. Spiritual principles and truths come from the Holy Spirit and are revealed directly to our spirit; He will use any available vessel even a child or a poorly educated street person.

Jesus said to the uneducated, unsophisticated, fisherman, Peter, *"flesh and blood has not revealed this unto you"* (Matthew 16:17).

The Holy Spirit revealed to Peter that Jesus was the Christ, Son of the living God. Whereas the educated Pharisees and Sadducees, who were the preachers and theologians of that day, were called whited sepulchers, vipers, blind leading the blind (Matthew 23:27). In fact, many times, the deepest principles in scripture are the simplest and sometimes our highly educated minds get in the way of receiving them as a little child, with childlike faith.

You will get a serious migraine headache if you try to figure God out. His thoughts are not your thoughts; His ways are not your ways. The way we think as women and the way many of us were trained to think about ourselves leaves us peddling around with foolishness compared to the wisdom and the truths of God. We are trained culturally to believe that women don't deal with the heavy spiritual, philosophical aspects of life, we're supposed to have babies, and make the meals while the men folk discuss the important issues of life.

Jesus said it like this in Luke 10:41 to Martha in answer to her question, *"Why don't you care that my sister has left me to serve alone, make her help me?"* *"Martha, Martha, thou art careful and troubled about many things: But one thing is needed; Mary hath chosen that good part, which shall not be taken away from her. She has chosen the living water which is eternal."*

If Jesus was at my house, teaching the truth that men sought for generations; God, <u>in my living room</u> revealing life, and I had the chance to sit at His feet, honey, folks would have had to go to McDonald's or Jesus would have to multiply some chicken wings. I would be right at His feet drinking the living water.

There will be times my sister, when the Father wants worship from you, and you may have to put the dish towel down and **give Him some praise!** Believe me; the dishes will still be there. Back to our Samaritan woman in John 4:11, she makes fun of Jesus *"You have nothing to draw with and the well is deep; where is this living water?"* She is on a different plane, not understanding at all.

In verse twelve she switches gears, finally realizing that He is talking about spiritual things, so she gets defensive about her religious group.

The second hindrance to worship is...

2. Religious Tunnel Vision

Whenever you say worship, each denomination, or religious group gets a list in his or her minds of what we do or don't do. We worship quietly, or we sing hymns, or we jump and shout, or we sing songs with rhythm. Worship is one of the main things God wants from people. Its way at the top of His list of reasons He created us! So, it is natural that Satan would bog down the issue with a lot of religious red tape.

The Samaritan woman gets an attitude with Jesus in verse twelve. "Well, who do you think you are? Are you greater than our Father Jacob who gave us the well?" If she lived in our times she might have said, "Rev Big Shot is our spiritual father, he gave us our worship do's and don'ts.

Jesus totally disregards her religious issues and goes right back to her need in verse thirteen. "...whosoever drinketh of this water that I shall give him, shall be in him a well of water springing up into everlasting life." She answers, "...give me this water, that I thirst not, neither come hither to draw."

She misunderstands the truth spoken, thinking He wants to meet a physical need.

The third hindrance to worship...

3. Focus on Physical Needs

Jesus is talking about spiritual water, a spiritual need. She says, fine; give me the everlasting water, so I don't have to keep coming to this well. Many of us come to the Lord because we think He will supply our physical needs; I need a husband, a new job, and a miracle. The Lord however consistently tells us to focus and prioritize on the spiritual. *"Seek ye first the kingdom of God and its righteousness and all these other things will be added unto you."*

The Father knows what you have need of. Matthew 6: 25: *"Take no thought what ye shall eat, or drink, or what ye shall put on."* This is the opposite of our nature—we want to be fed, clothed and comfortable.

The Father says, seek me first, I want to be first in your thoughts, your money, and the first fruit off the top. I want the first day of your week; come worship me first; love me with all your might, your energy and physical strength. I want your body, even while you're young; don't wait to get old and used up and then throw me the leftovers just in time to slide into heaven.

"I beseech you brethren by the mercies of God that you present your bodies a living sacrifice, holy, acceptable unto God." (Romans 12:1)

He wants your body holy. Single women; don't sleep with every man who buys you dinner. In fact, God tells you as a single woman you're free to focus on the things of the Lord.

The Bible states in I Corinthians 7:34: *"The unmarried woman careth for the things of the Lord that she may be holy both in body and spirit."*

Commit your way unto the Lord in everything you do acknowledge Him, and He will direct you. God even wants your children; He wants them trained in the nurture and the principles of the Lord because they are His heritage, not yours. Don't think this relationship with God is like a genie in a lamp or a heavenly Santa. Your needs get met in the process and there are even levels of abundance. However, Jesus was aware that some people only followed Him for the fish and loaves. Some thought, "He's giving out food, I'll be there". The Lord wants you to first focus on Him. Worship is about meeting His need, not yours.

In verse sixteen, Jesus tells her to call her husband. She honestly explains that she has none. That honest confession led to her spiritual quickening.

The fourth hindrance to worship:

4. Dishonesty with God

Be honest with God. Be quick to admit your sins. Don't make excuses: "Lord I did this because I was abused, ignorant, it's my parent's fault, and I was born this way, its part of my temperament. All the women in my family are like this." Excuses!

Before worship comes confession and before confession comes honesty with God. Sometimes, our prayers should sound like this: "Lord, I have sinned through disobedience, fear, worry, unbelief, depression, bitterness, anger, lust, adultery, fornication, lying, unforgiveness..." Be honest with God. Don't call sin by pretty names. You're not sexually active; you're committing adultery or fornication. Call it what God calls it. Don't rationalize your sin, "all the Smiths are like this." Don't rename it. You're not anxious, you're operating in fear; you're not being cautious, it's unbelief; you're not strong willed, you're rebellious; you're not spicy, you're bitter; you're not sharing a prayer need, you're stirring up strife. Be honest with God and yourself.

We tend to focus on manifest sins like smoking, drinking, and adultery. God, however, wants to get to the core of pride, rebellion, bitterness, anger, and fear.

Look at the list of things that God really hates. He calls them abominations in Proverbs 6:16. Three of them are not what we would expect: a proud look, one who stirs up strife, and a lying tongue. These are not the typical sins that we would put on our list of the "big sins", but God looks at the heart.

The Samaritan woman's honesty led her to her spiritual awakening. Jesus tells her about herself, exposes her sin and the truth sets her free.

The fifth hindrance to worship:

5. Making Men Our Gods

Women have a built in tendency to try and make men their god. We are taught from childhood to look for our Prince Charming, the one who will set us free. We are socialized to think life will just not be life without a man.

God says: "Thou shalt have no other gods beside Me." The Lord tells you He is a jealous God, when you worship, and put anyone or anything before Him. He visits the sins of the parents onto the children down three and four generations. We see this happening every day. Our children pick up our bad habits, temperaments, and sins; they do them worse than we did and our children double the negativity.

Finally, the Samaritan says, "I perceive that thou art a prophet." She tells him about her worship, but she focuses on the place of worship.

The sixth hindrance to worship:

6. Focusing On the Place

"We worship here and the Jews say we should worship in Jerusalem." She has moved up to a different level, dealing with deeper issues. She has come to the issue of worship but again gets bogged down in religious red tape. Jesus tells her it has nothing to do with the place. We call our churches a house of worship, yes, but some of us conclude that it is the only place to worship. If worship is a primary thing God wants, and He wants it all the time, how can we do that if we are locked into one location?

Primary Spiritual Truth

Verses twenty-three and twenty-four: *"But the hour cometh and now is, when the true worshiper shall worship the Father in spirit and in truth, for the Father seeketh such to worship Him in spirit and in truth."*

Worship is more than a physical response, an emotional outburst, or a thought pattern. It is the stretching of the very core of you, the deepest part of you, reaching to God, wanting with all your heart and soul to touch, embrace, and be enveloped by your Creator. You want what He wants—the coming of His kingdom.

It begins at your core, and then touches your heart (feelings), your mind, your will, and your body. You will want to be what He wants you to be, to serve Him and to make Him happy. This will be reflected in everything you do, not just your talk, but in your obedience. It is a lifestyle of worship.

What Is Worship?

The Bible says in Psalm 22:27: *"All the ends of the world shall remember and turn unto the Lord and all the kindred of the nations shall worship before thee. For the kingdom is the Lord's."*

1. Worship is required of everyone. It is universal.
2. Worship is focusing your thoughts, your heart, and attention on God, turning to Him.

The Bible says in Isaiah 45:22: *"Look unto me and be ye saved all the ends of the earth; for I am God and there is none other."*

The Bible says in Romans 14:11: *"For it is written, as I live saith the Lord, every knee shall bow to me and every tongue shall confess to God."*

<u>Give Him Your Attention</u>

Turn the T.V. off and give Him some quality time. I once participated in an "Information Fast" with a local church. We all committed to watch no T.V., except for the mews, and only watch Christian videos, movies and radio. We also chose whatever weekly food fast we felt led to do. Those hours that I usually spent watching T.V., were spent in prayer, worship, Bible study, reading Christian materials, and singing spiritual songs and hymns. I did this for forty days. It was an awesome time. God broke the T.V. stronghold in my life, my spiritual ears unclogged, and my relationship with God was forever changed. Even after the fast I knew I would never again be satisfied with the devotional life I had before; I missed the intimacy with God.

During that time the Lord gave me the answer to one of the problems I was having with my son for twelve years. All the doctors, psychologists, and neurologists didn't know what to tell us, but God whispered the answer to me in a quiet moment with Him. (Excuse me. I had to take a praise break just then. Even while I write about it, I think about His goodness and grace. Hallelujah!)

3. Humbling of self - bowing of heart, attitude, this will some-times be reflected by your body. Bowing of the head, on your knees or sometimes lying prostrate before Him (lying on your face). Remember that the emphasis is on the attitude. It is possible to bow with the knee and resist God in your heart, so don't get caught up with religious 'stuff.' You can bow the body and be saying in your heart, 'excuse me, I'm going to do what I want, God, I just have my eyes closed because everyone else does.'

This is not just the outward condition of where you are and how you are positioned. In spirit and in truth, your heart should say,

- 'You are God, I am not.
- You know what's best, I do not.
- You have all wisdom, power, and understanding. You are awesome, God!

If you believe those statements, you will order your life seeking Him about everything, choosing His direction, wanting to be what He wants. In other words, you will develop a lifestyle of worship.

<u>Lifestyle of Pride</u>

"I will pick my husband. I will choose my church. I will make all the decisions. 'I am woman, hear me roar.' I will pick my house and career. I will train my children in the way I think they should go…"

Now most of the time we don't consciously say this, but this is exactly what we do. Did you pray about all these decisions before you made them? Did you seek God's will, stand still and wait for His direction? These are all major decisions. Did you just marry the guy 'cause he was cute', or choose the church that had the nicest seats, or pick the house because it had the shutters you liked, or send your kid off to college to be a dentist because that was your dream?

It seems silly, but you would be surprised at how people make these major decisions.

This is a lifestyle of pride. God will humble you, and many times, towards the end of your life, after you have made a complete mess, you come to the altar realizing that God was just on the back burners in your lives. He was just your fire escape to miss the fire of hell, but you were the lord of your life. At the end of your life, you don't want to say, "I did it my way."

Lifestyle of Worship

"I will seek You in everything, Lord; You know what's best for me. You lead me to the right husband, career, friends, church and ministry. You are the Captain of my soul, the Lord and Sovereign God. Whatever you want me to do with my life, wherever you want me to go, I'm available. I will even seek Your face in the most insignificant details of life. Lord, lead me to the right dress. Reveal to me what is on Your heart."

When the physical show of worship comes out of that lifestyle and pattern of thinking, it's a part of worship.

Review:

1. Worship is required of everyone. (Every knee shall bow and every tongue shall confess...)
2. Worship is focusing your thoughts, your heart, and attention on God.
3. Worship is the humbling of self.
4. Worship is giving to God
    a. Adoration, praise
    b. Money
    c. Thanks
    d. Love

The Bible states in Deuteronomy 26:10: *"And now, behold, I have brought the first fruits of the land, which thou O Lord hast given me. And thou shall set it before the Lord thy God and worship before the Lord thy God."*

The Bible states in I Corinthians 16:29: *"Give unto the Lord the glory due unto his name: bring an offering and come before him; worship the Lord in the beauty of holiness."*

The Bible states in Psalm 95:6: *"O come, let us worship and bow down: let us kneel before the Lord our God our maker."*

How we worship depends on what we're giving:

Love or adoration may be very quiet, intensive, and intimate, or it may be joyfully ecstatic. This depends on how the Spirit is moving.

Money, thanks, and praise depends on how grateful you are. (There will be a different level and intensity if God blessed you with a new coat, or He just saved your drug addict son.)

Worship is not a mental thing, thoughtfully reading off a list of things you are thankful for. It is not even a soul thing, coming from your emotions or body. It starts in your spirit, but it turns on the faucet of the "rivers of living water," they flow from the inside out to your mind, emotions, and body. It will affect you on every level.

Worship is more a state of mind and a lifestyle, a complete surrendering of your whole being to God. Worship is progressive, as we offer all that we are and have to God; with maturity and obedience, He will show us pockets of resistance that we thought we had yielded. The more we are in His word and in His presence the more we become aware of areas of resistance. As we yield, we become more enveloped by His love, and we stretch from glory to glory. Just like the intimacy of a husband and wife is most precious in the private and quiet moments, even though they may hold hands or kiss in public likewise our most precious moments of intimacy with God will be in the quiet places, between you and Him.

Worshipping in spirit and in truth turns on the living water. That's what the Samaritan woman and we all really need. You can be in Bible school, memorize all the verses, do the papers and research and be dry as a bone. You can serve God with your body, on committees, work hard doing activities and be dry as a bone.

We come to church to worship as a group. However, your primary worship should be in your home. In church, we can't always wait for you to fall prostrate, or scream because the Spirit touched you, and you want to pour out your gratitude. You need to do those things, but in the group we have time constraints, an order of service; the needs of the group outweigh the needs of the individual.

God wants all types of worship and all your energy. Just read through the Psalms and understand all the levels of praise and worship demonstrated. We are commanded to sing, shout, dance, play instruments, clap our hands, raise our hands, bow down, kneel down, and cry out. There are times when the Holy Spirit will have you weep, mourn, repent, or do warfare in your spirit as you declare the Word with boldness to the forces of hell. Sometimes you will sit quietly in awe as you listen to the Lord correct you, instruct you, comfort you and love you.

There will be times when you are very alert as the Lord is warning you of an impending situation, trial or trap that your enemy has set. Every muscle in your body tenses with vigilance as the Lord gives you the alarm to begin to pray. Your loved ones may be in danger at that very moment and your prayer and intercession will be the deciding factor.

You will feel His heart, His love for people, His anger at injustice and wickedness, but ultimately His peace. His burdens are light and His yoke is easy because once you've prayed and followed God's instructions on a matter, and you are released. You don't have to keep carrying folk or worrying about them. Commit it to God in prayer, pray until you feel the release, and then leave the rest to God.

There is a difference between worship and praise. Praise begins with your body, some action. Notice these verses:

Psalm 47:1: *"Clap your hands oh ye people, shout unto God with the voice of triumph."*

Psalm 34:1: *"I will bless the Lord at all times, his praise will continually be in my mouth."*

Psalm 105:2: *"Sing unto him, sing psalms unto him, talk ye of all his wondrous worship."*

Psalm 149:3: *"Let them praise his name in the dance, let them sing praises unto him with the timbrel and harp."*

The Secret Place

We usually begin with praise. However, the more mature a Christian is the more he or she will be able to move right into worship. You must find that secret place spoken of in Psalm 91:1: *"He that dwelleth in the secret place of the Most High shall abide under the shadow of the Almighty."* Most folks have not taken up residence in the secret place; we learn to run in when we are in a crisis and then tip out when the storm passes over. However, God doesn't want you to just visit every now and then; He wants you to live there. It's secret because everyone doesn't know where it is. It's hard to find, but like a hidden treasure, when you find it, it is worth the effort. It's in this secret place that the supernatural protection plan of God kicks in.

Most Christians claim the promises in Psalm 91 but ignore the requirements they must fill, (dwelling in the secret place). Therefore, when something unpleasant happens to us, we are shocked. However, if we are honest with ourselves, we will admit that we were outside of the secret place, usually unaware of our enemy (Satan), and without any armor on. Now this does not mean that the Christian who is equipped, surrendered to God and vigilant will never go through any unpleasant or dangerous situation, but they will be so spiritually prepared, and even sometimes forewarned that the sting and horror are taken out of it. *"Many are the afflictions of the righteous but the Lord delivereth him out of them all."* Worshipping in spirit and in truth turns on the water—the living water. That's what the woman needed; that's what you need. Worship is the well springing up unto eternal life.

Quiet All Distractions

We must quiet the distractions to hear the Spirit of God; He usually speaks with a still small voice. This requires discipline. Yes, I said it, that bad word—discipline. However, in order to hear the voice of God and move into the secret place you must quiet your mind, your opinions, and your emotions. That's why God asks us to fast regularly, not to kiss up to Him because you didn't eat the chicken wings for three hours, but to learn to quiet your flesh (sin nature), ignore it, so you can focus on the spirit. You'll be able to hear His voice clearer; you need the practice of quieting yourself in your personal time with the Lord. That is why we need to start out with a specific time; it disciplines us to be consistent.

The goal is a prayer life. It takes a whole reorienting of your thought when you are praying all the time and living in the secret place. We must learn to focus on the spiritual realm because that's where things start.

If you were to look at the mirror and see a piece of hair sticking up the wrong way, you don't comb the mirror; you comb your hair, going to the root of the problem. Even though you see the problem in the mirror or the natural, the root is on your head (spiritual). This natural world that we see is just a reflection of what took place first in the spiritual realm. A wise woman doesn't comb at the reflection by fussing at the children, threatening to not cook or make Bubba sleep on the sofa. When there is a problem in her home, she goes to the source of the problem and begins to pray to see the changes needed. While your husband or children are sleeping you need to be praying. You need to be praying in the Spirit and making Biblical declarations about the situation instead of cussing folk out, nagging, screaming or throwing plates.

We are the only women on the planet that have the right, authority and privilege to impact the spiritual realm. The women of God can bind and loose things with their mouths and the Lord promises to bind and loose those same things in the heavens. As you spend time in His presence, He will direct you about what needs to be bound and loosed. A wise dweller of "Secret Place Street" will know this and immediately respond to the spiritual world with the appropriate response.

Benefits

You will get God's attention and approval. The Father is seeking, and looking for such to worship Him. The Bible didn't say He was looking for Bible students, although we should all be Bible students; He is not looking for workers, although we should all be workers. He is seeking worshipers. With His attention and approval come all His blessings. Worship ushers you into the presence of God and there are all kinds of treasure there.

The Bible says in I Chronicles 16:27: *"Glory and honor are in his presence, strength and gladness are in his place."*

The Bible says in Psalm 16:11: *"Thou will shew me the path of life, in thy presence is fullness of joy, at thy right hand there are pleasures for evermore."*

The Bible says in Exodus 33:14: *"And He said my presence shall go with thee and I will give thee rest."*

The Bible says in Isaiah 43:2: *"When thou passeth through the waters, I will be with thee and through the rivers, they shall not overflow thee, when thou walkest through the fire thou shalt not be burned, neither shall the flame kindle upon thee."*

Psalm 91 is basically a list of the protection afforded to those who abide in the secret place. It's a secret, not easy to find. It takes effort. Through worship, they have made staying in God's presence a lifestyle. These worshipers don't go now and then when they have a problem, but they take up permanent residence.

The Bible says in Psalm 91:14: *"Because he hath set his love upon me I will deliver him, I will set him on high, because he hath known my name he shall call upon me and I will answer, I will be with him in trouble, I will deliver him and honor him with long life. I will satisfy him and show him my salvation."*

The Bible says in II Corinthians 3:17-18: *"Now the Lord is that Spirit and where the Spirit of the Lord is there is liberty. But we all with open face beholding as in a glass the glory of the Lord changed into the same image from glory to glory even as by the Spirit of the Lord."*

Worship ushers you into the presence of God. In His presence are:

1. Glory
2. Honor
3. Strength
4. Gladness
5. Fullness of Joy
6. Path of Life—Your purpose
7. Pleasures for evermore
8. Rest
9. Protection—physical, emotional, spiritual
10. Liberty
11. Transformed into His image
12. Deliverance
13. Divine Response and Help
14. Long Life and Salvation

My sisters, God is calling you to press in and find your secret place under His shadow. Jesus patiently ignored the Samaritan woman's racial and religious attitudes, her shallowness and lack of understanding. He sees past her many husbands and adulterous relationships, all the way to her dry, hungry spirit, crying out for God, looking for love in all the wrong places. He speaks over and over to her need, until she catches the vision and says, "You are the Christ".

Jesus is looking past your stuff today: your attitudes, your distractions, your disobedience, your fear and your pain, all the way to your dry, hungry spirit. He is seeking you. He wants you to be a worshiper; one who will turn the T.V. off, get up a little earlier, and sometimes turn down your plate; one who will make going into His presence a priority and will seek the Kingdom of God first.

Will you turn everything over to Him? Will you really let Him be Lord in your life, not just your Savior? Will you humble yourself before Him regardless of what others do or don't do, giving Him the praise and worship that He deserves and desires? Everything you need or could ever want is waiting for you in His presence. Out of your belly will flow rivers of living water. He wants to turn on the faucet. There will not be any recognition or praise from man, no one will acknowledge you on the program or give you a plaque; however you will have power and intimacy with God and an unexplainable joy that will shake the world.

Pray this Prayer of Dedication:

Oh Lord, I want more of You. You have heard the cry from the depth of my heart, and I acknowledge that only You can fill the empty places inside. Please forgive me for putting people before You, for being distracted, fearful and not believing that You are all that I need. I believe that in You I live and move and have my being, You alone have the life, peace, hope and healing that I seek. I choose You to be my hope and expectation. Teach me to worship You in spirit and in truth. Fill me with Your Holy Spirit. In Jesus' name…glory… You're worthy… You're a good God… I bless You, I praise You Lord… (Take a little praise break and give Him some glory.) Amen!

Chapter 13

Satisfaction Guaranteed!

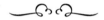

The words declared by God in Genesis 3:16 changed everything: *"...and thy desire shall be to thy husband, and he shall rule over thee.* This desire affects us today and also causes us problems. Since our husbands do not have the same desire we are often left feeling unsatisfied.

God put the desire for our husbands in us, but it usually feels like a curse because nowhere does it say that your husband's desire would be to you. The desire is not reciprocated. Now, you know ladies, that there is a difference between the love a man has for a woman and how we love them.

Have you ever thought or said: "God, I want to be loved, there is an emptiness inside. I had such hopes for this marriage; there is a longing down inside of me. I thought my husband would fill it. I thought my sweet little babies or my career would fill up this emptiness." **I can't get no satisfaction. "How** can I be satisfied in my marriage?"

Single women have been fooled into thinking that their dissatisfaction is just because they're not married. "If I could only get married I would feel fulfilled." If you have ever had any of these thoughts you're not alone. We say, "Ooh, praise the Lord, all is well," but down on the inside we're screaming, "I can't get no satisfaction!"

I'm going to share with you how you can find satisfaction because you will not be interested in meeting your husband's needs, nor will find total fulfillment as a single woman unless you learn where and how to get healed and fulfilled yourself.

Dissatisfied women who have or seek power can be dangerous because they will use their ability to influence in a destructive way.

I believe that God set up marriage as a system of protection for the woman. Men can be like bees, pollinating every pretty flower they see. Without the laws and restrictions of society, their natural tendency is to roam. When a woman is in love she will often go through hell for that man. It all goes back to that **desire** we have towards him. This desire creates two problems for us. First it is not reciprocated; second, he can't supply all we need.

There is no man on earth who can supply all your needs. You may be saying, *"Surely, Dr. Ja, Denzel or Brad could supply all my needs."* Not even Denzel or Brad, my sister, can supply all your needs.

Part of the purpose for the correctives in Genesis was to make men and women realize their need for God. God cursed the ground for man's sake, so he would have to spend his life working the ground, trying to bring life out of death. Adam and Eve originally tried to be like God, so God wanted them to know that they needed Him. Because Satan heard what God said to Eve, he quickly devised three lies to keep her from seeking God to fill her need.

Lie 1: The devil wants you to believe that a man can meet your needs. You know all your needs are not being met, therefore you conclude, *"If this man would only get it together, or maybe there is another man somewhere. I just married a lemon, a dud."*

Women always want more, which is why Satan can tempt them. We want the bigger house, more sharing, more intimacy, more romance, more...brother man, however, is content. When men are surveyed about their relationship, they usually rate satisfaction higher than their wives.

Three of the characteristics of women mentioned by Dr. Walker in his lesson, "Bone of My Bone; Male and Female Differences" were:

1. **Mentally inquisitive—a thirst for knowledge**
2. **Aesthetically perceptive—they like pretty things**
3. **Logically competitive—intellectually challenging**

<u>**Situation:**</u> You have this desire, you want more, and then I tell you no man can fill it. This means most women are frustrated, discontent and unfulfilled. I think that's why there are so many scriptures about contentious women. When our needs and expectations are not met we usually get contentious.

The Bible states in Proverbs 19:13: *"The contentions of a wife are a continual dropping."*

The Bible states in Proverbs 21:9: *"It is better to dwell in a corner of the housetop than with a brawling woman in a wide house."*

The Bible states in Proverbs 27:15: *"A continual dropping in a very rainy day and a contentious woman are alike."*

Some of our husbands know these verses by experience and the only reason they haven't left is due to the little bit of salvation they have. These same women say, *"He doesn't talk to me, we're not close, there's no romance."* Duh! Is your husband avoiding you, in church every night, staying at work, out with the boys, or hiding behind the newspaper? Is it possible that you have become contentious due to your frustration about unmet needs? You bought the lie that this man is to meet all your needs.

Lie 2: I put all my expectations on my husband. (Expectations are the things you long for, your intense anticipation, the thing you hope for.)

As single women we were told nonverbally and sometimes verbally that we were not complete until we were married and had children. The lie says *"you're not really satisfied until then."* So we dream and build all these expectations while we watch soap operas, love stories and dream of our wedding day. It began in childhood with nursery stories. Then we get married and after a few months, weeks, or sometimes days we inwardly ask, *"Is this it?"*

According to the Scriptures in Proverbs 13:12 (Amp): *"Hope deferred makes the heart sick."*

Many of us were disappointed because our hope was deferred, and we became heartsick. Well, then we think, ***"I know, I just need to have a baby, then I'll feel fulfilled."*** We have one or several, but that only complicates things. Now you have several "brats" hanging onto your dress and still feel frustrated and dissatisfied. There are some of us who can't have any children, and we spend the rest of our lives believing if I only had a baby everything would be all right.

Lie 3: That man is the total problem with this relationship.

Satan does not want you to see how you contributed to the problem, he wants you to put all the blame and focus on your husband so that God can't fix you. Satan wants you forever looking to a person for fulfillment because he knows you will be doomed to dissatisfaction. Let me give you some signs of dissatisfaction which can show up in a variety of ways in a woman's life.

Signs of Dissatisfaction

1. **Very Competitive**—must have the last word, must feel one up. Life is directed by her need to keep up with and surpass others.
2. **Complaining**—all the time
3. **Feeling of never having enough**—forty pairs of shoes, ten diamonds, and a house full of stuff. Buying things gives you a high.
4. **Out of balance in any area**—
   a. An overemphasis on career and ministry; neglects family.
   b. Children are your life; you try to keep them dependent even into adulthood.

    c. Husband is your life—"I can't live without him."

    d. Over focused on the outward- always in the mirror, spending a lot of your money on clothes, makeup, and hair.

5. Frequently controlled by negative feelings:

- Bitterness	- Despair	- Irritability
- Anger	- Fear	- Depression
- Anxious	- Insecurity	

6. Power Hungry—devious, manipulative, seeking to control others, starts mutinies in the church and on the job, stirs up strife, rebellion against authority. This sister will seduce and use her tongue. "By whatever means necessary" is her motto.

7. Sexual Promiscuity—Addictions, fornication, drugs, alcohol and even relationships.

8. Contentious, Brawling, Quarreling

<u>Worship Only Him!</u>

There is a place in our hearts fashioned specifically for God to fill. When we do not allow Him to fill that void we go about making other gods to fill it. We make idols. One of the idols in a lot of our lives is man. We have been acculturated from childhood to look for our Prince Charming, our hero, protector and savior. I've seen brilliant women with careers, jobs, homes, and cars give all they have for one fool who crosses their path, because he said, *"you all that baby girl."* She believes all his empty flattery and promises. I've seen women give up money, sex, and self respect for a few lies whispered in their ear. It is amazing what women will tolerate because... *"I love him, I can't live without him."*

That's an idol! Some of us will even take care of Bubba (financially) while he runs around and cheats on us and beats us to boot! There are women who lose all discernment and all their anointing goes out the window. They will rebel against pastor, parents and God Himself because some man kissed them on the neck. "He makes me feel like a woman" or "he makes me weak at the knees." Some will drop ministries, turn against family and even abandon their children to maintain his favor.

One woman turned on her seven-year-old daughter because her boyfriend was sexually abusing the child. She blamed the child and saw her as competition for her man. Some mothers in this situation just quietly ignore the abuse and live in denial; they turn their heads the other way for fear of losing that man.

Even mothers in the animal kingdom will take on a creature many times larger to protect her babies. However, some mothers will push their natural instinct aside because "*I can't live without him.*" He has become your idol!

You can also make your children idols. I know of a woman who moved to another state for years to be with her forty-year-old married son. She just left her husband to go and support her son. Career, money, clothes, cars, houses, your pastor, a rock star—any of these can be your god.

Idolatry! Not a word we use very often in this modern society, or if we do we are referring to some primitive society that worships idols. Realize that anyone or anything that we put before God in our lives is an idol to us. Think about these questions:

- What are the factors in your life that determine how you make important decisions and choices?
- Who do you seek out to guide you when you must determine the course your life will take?
- What do you think influences your major decisions the most: what your mama thinks, what your man thinks, your girlfriend, the needs of your children, what will best help your career, the opinions of the "in crowd", or God's will for your life? Don't lie! Be honest with yourself.

You'll find that most people put a whole bunch of other things before God. **Well, there are always consequences for idolatry.**

The Bible states in Jeremiah 17:5: "*Thus saith the Lord; cursed be the man that trusteth in man and maketh flesh his arm and whose heart departeth from the Lord. For he shall be like the heath in the desert and shall not see when good cometh; but shall inhabit the parched places in the wilderness in a salt land and not inhabited."*

DO YOU HAVE confidence in numbers or military strength physical strength, modern technology and discoveries.

The Bible states in Isaiah 31:1: *"Woe to them that go down to Egypt for help and stay on horses and trust in chariots because they are many and in horsemen because they are very strong; but they look not to the Holy One of Israel."*

Except the Lord keep the city, except He keeps you, the guard, the iron bars and pit bull are all in vain.

DO YOU HAVE confidence in your dreams, visions, emotions, cold sweats, heart palpitation, your logic, instinct or mother wit?

The Bible states in Proverbs 28:26: *"He that trusteth in his own heart is a fool."*

It is foolish, honey; your sin nature will deceive you. It works hand in hand with Satan to destroy you.

DO YOU HAVE confidence in your bank account, your job, union, tax broker, IRA, bonds and annuities, properties, stock or investments?

The Bible states in Proverbs 11:28: *"He that trusteth in his riches shall fall."*

DO YOU HAVE confidence in the men, the good ones, the princes, the finest, the wealthiest, the strongest and the smartest?

The Bible states in Proverbs 146:3: *"Put not your trust in princes nor in the son of man in whom there is no help."*

DO YOU HAVE confidence in the psychic network, Madam X, crystal balls, witchcraft, astrology, numerology, or spiritual advisors?

The Bible states in Isaiah 47:9: *"But these two things shall come to thee in a moment in one day, loss of children and widowhood, they shall come upon thee in their perfection for the multitudes of thy sorceries and the great abundance of thine enchantments for thou has trusted in wickedness."*

Nowadays we don't seem to connect the things we do contrary to God's Word with the consequences promised by His Word. What? Do you think God is kidding around when He says this stuff, or He's old and forgot He said it, or He'll make an exception for you? God is not playing, He has not changed, He didn't forget what He said, nor does it matter that you have not studied the Word and know what He says. Much of what we go through is **not** suffering for the name of Christ. We live such compromised lives that we rarely even disturb Satan. No, most of what we are suffering is for our violation of God's law's and commands. We are just reaping what we have sown. God watches over His word to perform it!

He Can Take the Weight

The only one who deserves our whole confidence is God. One day the Lord told me to sit in a chair and lean back and rest my whole weight on that chair, that's how He wanted me to lean on Him with my whole heart. We all have people in our lives that we can trust in varying degrees, but there is no one you can trust totally, at all times, without fail, but God.

Satan wants you out of balance!

The reason Satan wants you to put your confidence in anything or anyone other than God is because he has the sense enough to know that none of these things can hold you up. As soon as you lean upon them, they will fall. Why?

Because everything and everyone else can change but God never changes. He is the same yesterday, today and forever. His standards don't change. He doesn't get old or go out of style, nor does He have to be remodeled. He does not have to reconsider or review His opinions in light of recent developments. He sees all of time. He is not locked in time, but stands outside of it seeing it as a passing moment. He has given mankind a brief time to play out a drama directed, created, produced and featuring Him.

Leaning on other things throws you 'off balance'. According to Ephesians 6:12, we are wrestling against principalities, powers, rulers of darkness of this world, and wicked spirits in high places. In the sport of wrestling the main goal is to get your opponent off balance so he can be knocked down. In our relationships there must be balance. Our priorities must be in order. God gave you the order of your priority system.

Commandment One

The Bible states in Deuteronomy 6:5: *"And thou shalt love the Lord thy God with all thine heart, and with all thy soul, and with all thy might."*

Commandment Two

The Bible states in Matthew 22:39: *"And the second is like unto it, Thou shalt love thy neighbor as thyself."*

Notice that proper self-love comes before the love of other people. This is why we must focus on your own inner healing and contentment, which will make it easier for God to use you to bring healing and contentment to your husband and others. Let's look at God's plan to get satisfaction.

Pray this prayer of dedication:

Lord, I acknowledge that You in you alone I can put my trust. You alone are my hope and expectation. I will not lean on the arm of flesh. Because I trust in You, I will not be ashamed.

I know that in Your presence is fullness of joy. I thank You that You are filling the empty places in my life. Thank You for loving and drawing me even when I disobeyed and ignored You. While I was still a sinner You died for me. Please give me a hunger for more of You.

Chapter 14

How Do I Find Satisfaction?

The Plan

1. Repent for putting others before God
2. Recognize the Lie You Believed
3. Pull down the Stronghold with the Word
4. Redirect Your Desire
5. Become a Worshiper
6. Find God's Will for Your Life
7. Give and It Shall Be Given

Step 1: Repent

1. Repent: You must be in a position to receive from God, and to do that, you must repent. Realize that you have put other things and people before the Lord.

The Bible states in Hosea 10:12: *"Sow to yourselves in righteousness, reap in mercy, <u>break up your fallow ground, for it is time to seek the Lord,</u> till he come and rain righteousness upon you. Ye have plowed wickedness, ye have reaped iniquity, ye have eaten the fruit of lies, because thou didst trust in thy way in the multitude of thy mighty men, therefore shall a tumult arise among the people."*

What is fallow ground? It means freshly ploughed, to till the soil, break it up. How do you break up the hard, dry soil of your hearts so you can receive the seed of God's Word?

You must now:

a. **Abandon your idols** – put the Lord back in His place as the ruler of your life. Thank God if you have a good husband. Love him with the love of the Lord, but just acknowledge that God comes first in your life. (So if your husband asks you to do something illegal you would obey God rather than man.)

b. **Cleanse your temple** –Sweep out all the lies. Ask the Lord to cleanse your heart and forgive you.

c. **Return to the Lord** –Just make a decision to love the Lord with all of your heart, mind and soul. Make Him your priority. This will be a decision of your will not your emotions.

There is always a preparation for the things God wants to do with you.

- **No water for the army until they dug the ditches**. The Bible states in II Kings 3:16-17: *"Thus saith the LORD, Make this valley full of ditches. For thus saith the LORD, Ye shall not see wind, neither shall ye see rain; yet that valley shall be filled with water, that ye may drink, both ye, and your cattle, and your beasts."*

- **No oil until the vessels were gathered.** The Bible states in II Kings 2:3: *"Go borrow the vessels abroad of all thy neighbors even empty vessels, borrow not a few."* (Get ready for big blessings!)

- **No healing until the leper had dipped seven times in the river.** The Bible states in II Kings 5:14: *"Then went he down, and dipped himself seven times in Jordan, according to the saying of the man of God: and his flesh came again like unto the flesh of a little child, and he was clean."*

- **No reconciliation without repentance.** The Bible states in Isaiah 40:3: *"The voice of him that crieth in the wilderness,*

Prepare ye the way of the LORD, make straight in the desert a highway for our God."

Believe that God can fulfill and satisfy you! Take the time right now in the quietness of your heart to break up that hard, crusty soil of your heart. Even as you are reading, God wants, and longs to satisfy you. Be honest with yourself and Him. Confess that you have put other people and things before Him. Nobody can love you like He can. Take a moment now to open your heart to Him.

Step: 2 Recognize the Lie:

Realize which of the lies you have accepted. Check which one applies to you. Be honest.

Three Lies:

1. **A man can meet all my needs._____**
2. **My expectations are all or mostly in my husband._____**
3. **The man is the main problem._____**

These lies come from Satan. Lies that are believed and accepted become the foundation for strongholds upon which Satan builds other lies. The devil is very patient my sister, he has been around for many years. He is willing to begin with a very small, false concept. He knows he can expand on that thought and slowly, quietly increase his hold, killing you gradually.

If you've bought the lie that a man will meet all your needs, as soon as the honeymoon cloud lifts, you begin to realize that you don't feel fulfilled. You begin to put pressure on your husband. *"Spend more time with me. You don't tell me you love me. There's not enough intimacy. It's not like it was when we were dating..."*

You have bought the lie that your husband is the source of your happiness, all your dreams, hopes and future when everything revolves around him in some way. It may be something that you have never verbalized, but when you think about your life, your actions speak louder than words. If you feel no joy except when he is around, or if you feel no value except when he says you're acceptable, if you're willing to tolerate any type of abuse, cruelty, meanness, and selfishness because you love him, and you can't live without him, you bought the lie, hook, line and sinker!

Now, depending on the man, he may try harder to please you and end up frustrated, or he may withdraw more. This can lead to nagging and arguments.

He may avoid you and even walk out if he can't take the pressure. You may begin to envy others, looking around at other men. There is a host of ways the enemy can take these problems and turn them into greater danger for the marriage, depending on your weaknesses as individuals and as a couple.

Scenario:

Here are examples of what line of thinking the enemy can lead you into:

Lie: *This man is your husband; he's supposed to meet all your needs; what good is a marriage if you don't feel satisfied? You've just missed the boat; maybe if you had married George... he understood you, give him a call, he was so easy to talk to...and I heard his marriage wasn't going so well. Maybe you can encourage each other...*

Male response: *That woman is really pressuring you man. She always wants more. Don't you feel boxed in? Your boys told you it would be like this. She nags you all the time. Susan, your secretary, is a good listener; she doesn't pressure you. She's got nice legs too. Call her; she'll listen to your problems...*

These are examples of possible conversations we have in our minds between our flesh (sin nature), and the devil. His job is to encourage our flesh to consider these options, rationalize our evil thoughts which if not rejected can move us to evil actions. It's a very slow, subtle process. It is a very individual process depending on your weaknesses, how far the devil can take you, how spiritually mature you are, how well rooted you two are in the Word. The possible scenario indicated that these two might be headed for adultery. This may not be your weakness. Satan may know that he couldn't get you to do that, so he may tempt you with alcohol, gluttony, divorce, depression, backsliding, violence or any number of other negative responses to dissatisfaction and marital pressures.

One lie leads to a whole series of problems.

Step 3: Pull Down the Stronghold

Once you repent, recognize the lie, and then you must pull it down. You fight lies with truth. You can sometimes tell how deeply rooted the lie is by the amount of resistance you have against the truth. If as you are reading this you are coming up with all types of rationalizations in your mind, you may feel irritated, or you have a battery of excuses for yourself, you probably have some degree of a stronghold established.

A stronghold is just a **fortified place of defense, our defenses against the Word of God.** The older you are, usually the more established and elaborate the stronghold. I have talked to women who had such a strong line of defense against certain portions of God's truth that when you talk to them about it, they actually shut down and don't hear what you are saying. They may say "Uh huh," but their conversation tells me, she didn't hear or understand a word I said.

Satan has a vested interest in us not hearing the Word of God. You can sing, shout, serve on the usher board, cook the chicken and not disturb the enemy at all, as long as you don't hear some truth that will actually make changes in your life. The baby will cry, you'll get so sleepy, or you'll be daydreaming about your new dress right at the point of the message that you need to hear.

That is why God said give the most earnest heed to the things that you hear, lest at any time you let them slip. God's Word dispels Satan's lies.

"Well, Sister Walker, doesn't my husband have a responsibility to meet my needs, what's the point of being married?" Yes, he has a God given responsibility, but the only person you are accountable for is you. He has a free will. He may not fulfill what God requires of

him, and he may be ignorant of his responsibility or too bound to do it. God holds you responsible to do what He told you to do regardless of anyone else. Besides, I'm not talking to him, I'm talking to you!

The Bible states in Psalm 62:5: *"My soul, wait thou only upon God, for my expectation is from Him."*

The Bible states in Psalm 62:1: *"Truly my soul waiteth upon God; from Him cometh my salvation."*

Salvation, translated from the Hebrew means: He is my deliverance, my aid, victory, prosperity, health, help, saving, welfare.... He is all of that. Paul said, "For me to live is Christ," not for me to live is Joe. Many of us build our whole lives using a man as our foundation. I would remind myself as a young, single woman when I sang, "My hope is built on nothing less than Jesus blood and righteousness, I dare not trust the sweetest frame (that fine man I was dreaming about was the sweetest frame) but wholly lean on Jesus name."

Supernatural Peace

When a husband leaves, any woman will be hurt deeply, but some will recover and go on with their lives while others will hurt way down in their spirit and never recover because their foundation, their stability and hope is totally gone. It is totally natural and understandable that the betrayal of a spouse would devastate anyone, but when you hurt in body, mind and emotions, they can heal with time. God can even supply a special balm, a supernatural unexplainable peace that passes all understanding. In other words, it won't make sense. It will baffle you, your enemies, and your friends. That peace is like a shield and protection.

The Bible states in Philippians 4:6-7: *"Be careful for nothing (**don't worry**) but in everything by prayer and supplication with thanksgiving let your request be made known unto God and the peace of God which passes all understanding will keep your hearts and mind through Christ Jesus.*

That peace is to rule your heart.

The Bible states in Colossians 3:15: *"And let the peace of God __rule__ in your hearts."*

Rule means to umpire, govern, and prevail. When peace is governing and prevailing in your heart you make decisions based on God's point of view. Things that seem catastrophic and life ending from our perspective are just a part of the puzzle that comes up good in the end. All things are working together for your good if you love God and are the called according to His purpose.

Our time here is temporary, short, like a vapor. God's opinion of us is eternal. We can no longer live by our emotions; we must live by the Word.

Once our spirit is wounded, the Word says a wounded spirit, who can bear it? These are the women who have made man the foundation of their lives. If that foundation leaves, dies or betrays her, she can become suicidal, have a nervous breakdown, go into abnormally long periods of depression or become addicted to something.

The Bible states in Jeremiah 17:5: *"Thus saith the Lord; cursed be the man that trusteth in man and maketh flesh his arm, and whose heart departeth from the Lord"*

The Bible states in Psalm 18:8: *"It is better to trust in the Lord than to put confidence in man."*

I'm convinced that one of the reasons God called David a man after His own heart was that David knew who to put his trust in. Read through Psalms, and highlight every time you see "I will trust in the Lord" or some similar phrase. Your man and no other man can meet all your needs. Most of the time he's more messed up than you.

Picture what this may look like in the spirit realm.

Spiritual wounds	Chains of generational bondage
Strongholds	Defensive
Roots of bitterness	Stripped of Power

We turn our backs on God who has everything we need, and all we can see is that man. You beg him to give you all the love and security you missed in childhood, you cry out, please love me and make me whole! Do you see how foolish this is? Whenever Satan is trying to feed you the lie, allow the Word to correct you. The Word is your standard for truth, not Joyce Brothers or the survey in Cosmo.

Review the first three steps to satisfaction

1. Step 1 - Repent
2. Step 2 - Recognize the lie
3. Step 3 - Pull down the stronghold with the Word

Assignment:

- Sit down now and write out the lies that you have accepted to whatever degree. Since you started reading this book the Holy Spirit has probably pricked your heart several times about thoughts you've had. Even if you've just believed it a little bit, or if you say you don't believe it, but your actions seem to indicate that you might.
- Next, write down the scripture that refutes the lie. It could be some scripture that I have already quoted, or a scripture that the Lord brings to your remembrance, or you may need to look in the concordance of your Bible and find scriptures that will cancel the lies.

<u>Example:</u>

Lie - My husband is the whole problem/ Truth – *Romans 3:23: "For all have sinned and fallen short of the glory of God."*

Truth - *I John 1:10 - "If we say that we have not sinned we make Him a liar, and the truth is not in us." Matthew 7:3-5 - "And why beholdest thou the mote that is in thy brother's eye but considerest not the beam that is in thine own eye... Thou hypocrite, first cast out the beam out of thine eye; and then shalt thou see clearly to cast out the mote out of thy brother's eye."*

I could go on and on. Scripture clearly teaches the wisdom of self-examination, not to compare ourselves with other people because our standard is to be like Jesus. It will take all of your focus to allow your sin nature to die and let Christ live through you. You will have very little time to try and play the role of the Holy Spirit for your husband.

By the way, this is a powerful way to re-indoctrinate yourself with regards to **any** of the lies Satan has rooted in your mind.

You need to be very aware of them for this is where the battle-ground is. If you have a poor self-image due to things said to you as a child, look up Scripture that cancels the lie, memorize it, and say it when you have those negative thoughts. Actively use the Word as a weapon to fight the mind attacks of the devil. When Jesus was tempted by Satan in the wilderness, He didn't give His church affiliation; He fought back with **"It is written."** He slammed the Word in the devil's face.

If he tells you "you are weak," tell him and yourself, "I am more than a conqueror through Christ." If he whispers, "you're stupid," tell him "I have the mind of Christ." If he says "you're not going to have enough money," shout, "The Lord will supply all of my needs according to His riches in glory."

Always be aware of how you're thinking. Is it consistent with the Word or is it something you got out of a magazine or the lyrics to a song? This is why God wants us to yield every thought.

The Bible states in I Corinthians 10:4, 5: *"For the weapons of our warfare are not carnal, but mighty through God to the pulling down of strongholds, Casting down imaginations, and every high thing that exalteth itself against the knowledge of God, and bringing into captivity every thought to the obedience of Christ."*

Step 4: Put Your Expectation on God

Take all of that desire, yearning, hope, dreams, and expectations and turn it to God. Focus on God. Now this requires mental and spiritual discipline. Your natural tendency is to blame everything on the man or the devil. So when you start thinking, *"If he would just get his act together, maybe if I threaten to leave or not cook or make him sleep on the sofa,"* **Stop. Rewind,** *"It's me, oh Lord standing in the need of prayer."* Focus on you and God, *"I am trusting You Lord, You are my hope and expectation, and You are the strength of my life. You are the only one who cannot fail; You are my hope of glory."*

Put all your expectations on the Lord. Even the best of men will fail you at times, which is the very nature of being human. The sooner you understand this, the happier you'll be. Many times God will orchestrate a number of failures and disappointments so that you will finally realize **He** is who you need.

These are some examples of daily declarations you need to make:

God, I'm trusting in You to supply all of my needs according to Your riches. I am trusting in You. You are my hope and expectation. No matter what happens, I can live because it is in You that I live, move and have my being. I can solve my problems today by Your wisdom. You said if I need wisdom, I could ask of You, and You would give liberally. I have the mind of Christ.

No weapon formed against me will work today and I condemn every tongue that rises up against me. No negative words will hinder me because Your Word, Lord, is truth. It tells me that I am blessed going in and out, sitting down and rising up.

You look up Scriptures that will fit your situation. Now while you are focusing on God, He's getting the mess out of you.

Fear	**Rebellion**
Nagging	**Critical Tongue**
Insecurity	**Anger**
Contention	**Bitterness**

As you focus on God, you draw on the blessings of God, and He begins to satisfy you. God wants to satisfy you.

The Bible states in Psalm 63:1-2, 5: *"O God, thou art my God, early will I seek thee: my soul thirsteth for thee, my flesh longeth for thee in a dry and thirsty land, where no water is: To see thy power and thy glory, so I have seen thee in the sanctuary. My soul shall be satisfied as with marrow and fatness: and my mouth shall praise thee with joyful lips."* (KJV)

Your husband has barriers of his own and strongholds that can keep him from receiving God's love or your love. These barriers can also keep him from giving you the love you need. So even if you're not receiving from your husband, God wants to love you through him. He may be blocked. Any love that is coming from your mate is ultimately from God; the man is just a vessel. All good and perfect gifts are from above and God is love personified.

Remember, the source is God. If He can't channel it through your husband; He can go another way. The closer your relationship is with God the more He can directly minister love to your heart. If you do not have a well-developed relationship with God, He will still use others to express His love. You may not yet be able to hear or discern the voice of God. (Yes, He still speaks today, and not just through your pastor).

You may be so wounded you are unable to receive and believe God's love for you. You're like a bag with holes. The holes represent wounds in your heart. God's love flows into your heart, but out through the holes of woundedness, ignorance and Satan's lies about God. There may be strongholds of rejection (*God couldn't love me*), or condemnation (*I don't deserve to be loved*).

If you have a wounded heart, and you have a hard time receiving God's love, perhaps due to abuse as a child, or rejection by parents, there are several things you must do:

- Get into a Bible-teaching church.
- Get as much of the Word as possible—Sunday school, Bible class, books, tapes.

Try to not become overly dependent on people. If you were abused in childhood, there is a tendency to be drawn to other people who will abuse you. There are some people in ministry and the helping, counseling fields that will take advantage of you. So get good references really seek the Lord and try to get a good, basic foundation in the Word.

It takes a steady hearing of the Word through teaching, preaching, and memorization to heal the holes in your soul. You need to understand and experience the unconditional love that loves the real you, with the good and the bad; a love that won't go away if you gain weight, change, age, or just blow it; A love that reaches down into the depths of your sin, your drunkenness, adultery, rage, bitterness, fear and hate. It pulls you up, cleans you off, sets you on a solid, unmovable foundation, and calls you royal, accepted in the beloved, joint heir, and child of God.

There is no greater joy than to hear the voice of God saying, "I love you daughter." He's not just talking to the world with some universal, general, global love; He is addressing you personally, baby. You are precious to Him;

- "I love you with an everlasting love; my thoughts of you are good and not evil. I want you to prosper and be in good health even as your soul prospers. I want to give you the desires of your heart and an abundance you can't even imagine. Because I love you, yes you, I know your quirks and the very worst of you, but My blood shed on Calvary covers you and makes you righteous and beautiful to Me."

Can't nobody beat His rap; it's steady and true and He's got the power to back it up. He is the lover of your soul, He is a faithful lover; He loved you first and saw the best in you when you were worthless. He won't see someone else two years from now and go off and leave you. He is faithful.

The Bible says in II Corinthians 5:21: *"For he hath made him to be sin for us who knew no sin; that we might be made the righteous of God in him."*

Take for example, the woman caught in the very act of adultery. Jesus silences the accusers, He does not want you to live in guilt, beaten down, and feeling like you'll never be good enough. *"For by one offering he hath perfected forever them that are sanctified."*

Your Deepest Need Is In Your Spirit

There are three areas of need in a woman's life; **body, soul,** (will, emotions, mind) and **spirit.** If you are a born again believer your spirit is where God dwells. Way down on the inside of us our spirit has certain needs. Your spirit is crying out for God. That is the deepest, most persistent need you have because your spirit is eternal. It is at the core of your being, it is the most important part of you. We tend to want to begin and end with our physical and emotional needs. Most of us believe our emotional needs are the most important. As long as we feel good, honey chile, we think that's it.

We often confuse our need for God as one that can be filled with human love, sex, marriage, babies, a career, a degree, power, influence, beauty, a new diamond, a fur coat...We sing Jesus you're my everything, all I need is Jesus, but you always seek after the thing that your heart craves the most. I'll say it another way: we know where your heart is based upon what you seek after. We don't usually seek after God, unless we're in a crisis. Most of us spend major time getting the attention, approval, and affection of people.

If you get all the things you want, you will still feel unfulfilled if you don't satisfy your spiritual man.

Sometimes folk who have everything realize this way ahead of the rest of us. When you're one of the "have-nots" you keep thinking there is something, somewhere that will fill you, I just have to find it.

I remember seeing a report on T.V., years ago about a county in California that was the richest county in the U.S. They also had the highest rate of divorce, suicide and addictions. What do you do when you get to the end of the rainbow, and it's not enough?

Stop wasting time. God created you. He tells you that you were created to fellowship with Him, to live and abide in Him. If you're not doing that, you're going to feel unfulfilled. Salvation doesn't automatically develop fulfillment, it only opens the door. You've got to go into the throne room, sit down and get to know your God. That has nothing to do with Christian service, ministry, singing in the choir or giving to the church.

The heart of God yearns and longs for your fellowship, love, worship and intimacy, He has always wanted to have a people who love him voluntarily. He would be their God, and they would be his people. He says, "Come, let us reason together." He went to extreme measures to regain fellowship with us. He knew He could not make a covenant with sinful man, so He became man and made a covenant with Himself. Then He put us "in Christ", so we would be a part of it. We were crucified, buried, and resurrected with Him, so we could be in fellowship again.

The Bible says in Jeremiah 31:3: *"I have loved thee with an everlasting love..."*

Our God loves intimacy. He is not asking for a casual relationship. He doesn't want, "Hey God, bless me, fix me, see ya next Sunday." He doesn't want a relationship that is forced. He gave us a free will, so we could choose Him. ("Whosoever will, he that hath an ear, if any man...") Even after we choose Him, He still gives us choices. "I set before you this day an open door, choose life."

Some will have a harvest of thirty, sixty, or one hundred fold. It depends on how much you are willing to invest in the kingdom of God. You can have power in God, it depends on if you're willing to pay the price.

God Wants Intimacy

If you quench the Holy Spirit, or grieve Him, He will pull back. Do you realize that you're in a relationship with a God who loves you so much that He can be grieved (have his feelings hurt) by you? You better be glad I'm not God. God has chosen the most intimate human relationship to explain our relationship to Him: father, husband, mother, brother, and friend.

Father— Romans 8:15 says: *"For ye have not received the spirit of bondage again to fear; but have received the Spirit of adoption whereby we cry Abba (Hebrew for papa, daddy) Father."*

This is not just a formal relationship you have with a distant father, but it implies an intimate, close relationship where you address him as, "Daddy."

Mother— Deuteronomy 32:11-12 says: *"As an eagle stirreth up her nest, fluttereth over her young, spreadeth abroad her wings, taketh them, bear them on her wings, so the Lord alone did lead him."*

El Shaddai—One of the names of God. The Greek term for female (*Thelius*) means 'breasted one'. The name female corresponds to the *El Shaddai* name of God. *Shaddai* comes from the Hebrew word *'Shad'* which means 'big breasted one, mother nurturer, strength giver, satisfier, and the one who is enough." So, *El Shaddai* means: the Almighty big breasted, all sufficient, satisfying God who is enough. Glory to God, girl, He is enough!

Husband—Ephesians 6:23, 25 says: *"For the husband is the head of the wife, even as Christ is the head of the church: and he is the Savior of the body. Husband, love your wife,* **even as Christ also loved the church, and gave himself for it."**

Even Closer—Ephesians 5:30 says: *"For we are members of his body, of his flesh, and of his bones."* HOW CLOSE IS THAT?

The love of the Lord is the intimacy you long for, the total acceptance, the enveloping pure love that lasts forever; it is the love we sing about in love songs. The brothers don't have it, and they can't do it.

The Bible states in Psalm 16:11: *"Thou will shew me the path of life; in thy presence is fulness of joy, at thy right hand are pleasures for evermore."*

Emotional Needs

After you get your spiritual needs met there are valid emotional relationship needs that we have as women. Once you stop confusing your intense spiritual needs with your emotional ones, it takes a lot of the sting out of your true emotional needs. However, even in this area, God is your source. He uses human vessels to satisfy these needs. He can use your husband, children, parents, friends, prayer partners and the general body of Christ. This is why we are asked to love one another, rejoice and weep with each other, be kind, tenderhearted, forgiving, gentle, etc. This type of loving, accepting Christian community should go a long way in making us feel cared for and supported. However, if folk don't do what they're supposed to do, God is still your source.

My husband and I are ultimately responsible for feeding our children. We may leave them with a babysitter, but we must make arrangements for them to be fed at that time. We are their source of sustenance. Likewise, God is our source of satisfaction; He will use your husband, children or a variety of other vessels, but He is your source.

Our area of greatest need, other than spiritual, is emotional. Men are usually weakest at fulfilling these needs. They are weak in the area of loving, so God commands them to love us. So, it is likely that your husband is not meeting all your emotional needs, but even if he is a closed vessel, God is able to find other people to meet your emotional needs. Also, many of our emotional needs are met as we grow stronger in our relationship with God. As He fills us with the Holy Spirit we experience peace, joy, security, healthy self-love, confidence, and encouragement. As we fill the condition that goes with the promise (there is always a condition we must fill) the Lord promises to remove fear, hopelessness, loneliness, weakness, and depression. Jesus is the cure for whatever ails you.

Physical Needs

The third area of need is your body: the physical need for sex, to be held, cuddled, kissed and touched. Of course, God uses your husband exclusively for your sexual needs and He made it his responsibility. Your husband is supposed to fulfill this need, according to the scripture, only withholding it if either of you are fasting. (Well, looking at the condition of the world, there are obviously not too many people fasting and praying, so you should at least be having fun.)

Usually, the brothers don't put up much of a fight and are glad to meet the physical need, however, there are some instances where this is not the case. In those cases where your husband is not meeting your sexual needs, you will need to channel your sexual energy into exercise, housework, sports or creative arts. Don't let the devil tell you that you can't live without sex and then give you an excuse to have an affair. Work on the other aspects of your relationship, sex only reflects the problems in the other parts of your relationship.

In the meantime, the Lord can use others to kiss, cuddle and hold you, such as parents, children, and friends. Godly, appropriate affection takes place in the church as we greet one another with a godly hug. (No body slamming the brothers!) You know what I'm talking about, feeling unfulfilled and some cute evangelist comes to town and you sorta heave your body up on him when you hug him and thank him for his message which inspired you so much. Sorry I mentioned it; I know you would never do that.

In all these areas remember who your source is; and when the supply is cut off, don't waste time screaming at the vessel, go to the source. God knows what you have need of even before you ask. He made you; he created your sexuality and every other part of you. If your water supply was cut off you would not spend the day beating and cursing the pipes, you would call the water company. How do I get God's attention? Pray His promises to Him.

The Bible states in Psalm 103:5: *"Bless the Lord, oh my soul... who satisfieth my mouth with good things so that thy youth is renewed like the eagle."*

This is how you pray the promise: **Lord, I bless You with all that is within me. You satisfy my mouth with good things so that my youth is renewed like the eagle. Therefore, instead of moaning all the time, "nothing good happens to me, I am so unhappy, I am old and falling apart," speak life instead of death. Here are some additional promises you can pray for satisfaction.**

The Bible states in Psalm 107:9: *"For he satisfieth the longing soul and filleth the hungry soul with goodness."*

The Bible states in Isaiah 58:11: *"And the Lord shall guide thee continually and satisfy thy soul in drought and make fat thy bones..."*

The Bible states in Jeremiah 31:14: *"And I will satiate the soul of the priests with fatness, and my people shall be satisfied with my goodness, saith the Lord.*

The Bible states in Psalm 63:5: *"My soul shall be satisfied with marrow and fatness: my mouth shall praise thee with joyful lips."*

The Bible states in Psalm 16:11: *"Thou wilt shew me the path of life: in thy presence is fullness of joy, at thy right hand there are pleasures for evermore."*

God watches over His word to perform it. He longs to fellowship with you and that is exactly what you need.

Step 5— Become A Worshiper!

You need to be a worship expert. I don't care if you belong to a church that won't even say "Amen." God expects you to be a worshiper. The best place to worship is in your quiet place at home.

We're supposed to go to church to worship, but many churches have no idea of what it is. You don't even have to be loud. My most intimate times with God are usually when I am the quietest, listening to him speak to me or me loving him from the deepest part of me, usually with tears and a silent cry.

Praise and Worship

First you must know how to praise the Lord... The Bible states in Psalm 9:11: *"Sing praises to the Lord."* The Bible states in Psalm 33:2: *"Praise the Lord with harp, sing unto him with psaltery."* The Bible states in Psalm 67:3: *"Let the people praise thee."* The Bible states in Isaiah 42:12: *"Declare his praise in the islands."*

The Bible states in Hebrews 13:15: *"By him therefore let us offer the sacrifice of praise to God continually that is the fruit of our lips."*

The Bible states in I Peter 2:9: *"But ye are a chosen generation... that ye should shew forth the praises of him."*

The Bible states in Psalm 35:28: *"And my tongue shall speak of thy righteousness and of thy praise all the day long."*

Scripture goes on and on telling us to praise the Lord all the time, everywhere, and in every situation. It does not say just sing a few praise songs in church on Sunday but Scripture describes a praising lifestyle. Sometimes you don't feel like it, and then you offer the sacrifice of praise. "Lord I will praise you anyhow."

You offer all kinds of praise. The Word says to praise with song, praise with your mouth, praise with a loud noise, clap your hands, dance before the Lord, and use the instruments, just to name a few.

These are some of the words translated praise in the Old Testament that shows the different types of praise:

Yadah—To hold out the hand, with extended hands.

Halah—To make a show, to boast, to be clamorously foolish, to rave....

(Some say, "It doesn't take all of that," yet they'll do exactly that at the football game, or for a movie star or a singer. God deserves to have us rave or boast and be clamorous over Him.

Tehillah—a hymn
Zamar—to give praise on an instrument (Psalm 21:13)
Towdah—extension of hands, a choir of worshipers (Jeremiah 17:26)
Shebach—to adore (Daniel 4:34)
Shabach—to address in a loud voice, to command (Psalm 147:12)

Now, worship is on a deeper level. Jesus told the woman at the well that the Father was seeking worshipers, those that would worship in spirit and in truth. Worship is intimacy with God. The analogy the Lord gave us is a bride and a bridegroom, the most intimate human relationship. The Lord is the lover of your soul and worship is your intimacy time with God.

A worshiping woman is a satisfied woman. The Lord can touch you where no one else can. Your spirit was made to worship Him, and you must take the time to get to know Him. Learn His voice, learn His Word, seek Heart, seek His will, and learn what pleases Him and what upsets Him. Spiritual hearing is developed by a life of obedience. The more obedient you are to the Lord, the more your spiritual ears will tune in to His frequency.

Do even the little things God tells you, if you are faithful in the little, He will make you ruler over much. Obedience unclogs our spiritual ears. In the spiritual realm, God will open up dimensions you never knew existed and satisfy you with pleasures forever more.

Step 6: Find God's Will for Your Life

Knowing why you were created and what God has for you to do, will bring a sense of fulfillment. There is something He has for you to do as an individual and as a couple. After that is clear, then you need to know what God is doing in the body of Christ and His purposes in the world. We're living in exciting times, and there is satisfaction, peace and excitement that comes with knowing God's will and being in the flow. God is preparing us to rule this earth. He wants us to have dominion on the earth, to get back what Adam lost.

The Bible states in Romans 8:19-20: *"For all creation is waiting eagerly for that future day when God will reveal who his children really are. Against its will, everything on earth was subjected to God's curse. All of creation waits with eager longing for God to reveal his sons. For creation was condemned to lose its purpose, not of its own will... yet there was the hope that creation itself would one day be set free from its slavery to decay and would share the glorious freedom of the children of God."* (NLT):

You have to stop just looking at this world with its cares, pressures and hopelessness. As a child of God you need to be focused on the spiritual realm.

The Bible states in II Corinthians 4:18: *"While we look not at the things which are seen, but at the things which are not seen."*

If you focus on the temporal, temporary view of this world you will get sucked into the hopelessness. All that was created is groaning and waiting for the manifestation of the sons of God to be revealed.

What is God doing? Have you noticed that He's bringing the Body of Christ together? There is a great move of revival going on in some places in the world. Many are seeing miracles, healings and an increase of the supernatural. There is less debate over doctrinal issues and more commonality is being emphasized.

There is a return to God by the black middle class; times are so hard that everyone seems to know that we are living in the last days, even the unsaved. Movie stars, sports heroes and singing sensations are turning to God, even singing about Him in their songs. There are programs about miracles and angels on television all the time.

There is also a reaction and escalation of Satan's kingdom. Witchcraft is openly being advertised on television through the psychics. Every other show is about aliens, ghosts, and the unexplained. The world used to laugh at anything not scientific, but now it is rather chic to explore the paranormal. The enemy desensitizes the younger generation to the demonic realm by filling the cartoons, movies, videos and reading materials with witches, warlocks, gargoyles and demons. There is also an increase of people moving into devil worship, crystals, fortune telling, meditation and séances.

There is a spiritual war going on. Each side has increased the stakes with eternal repercussions, and all you can think about is which chicken recipe to cook for dinner, or that your husband won't talk to you.

If you ever get your eyes on the broader picture, find out what you're supposed to be doing to further the kingdom the God. You won't have so much time to get depressed over your problems. You take care of God's business, and He'll take care of yours. Seek first the kingdom of God and all its righteousness and all these other things that you worried about will be taken care of. Many times when I'm feeling sorry for myself the Lord will let someone call who needs my help and counsel. After I finish encouraging them, I feel better.

Finally, knowing God's purpose for you as a couple can really strengthen, focus, and spice up a marriage. You will begin to see yourself as a team, working together; that is usually part of God's plan. As you help your husband to fulfill God's will for his life, you get blessed. It gives you something to focus on, talk about and be excited about together.

Step 7: Give and It Shall Be Given Unto You

Give and it shall be given unto you...sowing and reaping is a kingdom principle that affects everything, not just your finances. Whatever you sow you reap. Learn to sow what you want, sow love, acceptance, and peace, and they will come back to you. Usually when our husbands don't do what we want, we begin to sow bitterness, anger, strife, jealousy, fear, and then we wonder why we get a harvest of the same stuff. Then of course we sow more negative seeds, locking us into a negative cycle.

Dr Clarence Walker shares "do you know why we reap what we sow? It's because we sow what we reap. We take the seeds from the harvest that just came in, sow them and the cycle begins again." Thank God, He interrupts this cycle by giving us new seed to sow.

The Bible states in II Corinthians 9:10: *"Now he (God) that ministereth seed to the sower both minister bread for your food, and multiply your seed sown, and increase the fruits of your righteousness."*

We are to sow to righteousness; the fruits of the Spirit are love, joy, peace, longsuffering, gentleness, goodness, faith, meekness and temperance. God is looking to see these fruits in you, in the way you treat your husband and children.

This is not just a nice list of words we put up on the Sunday school wall. It's funny how some of us try to be all deep and spiritual and miss the simplicity of what God wants. **Treat the man right, get your hand off your hip, and stop cussin' him out and talking about his mama. Stop cutting him up, tearing him down, ridiculing him and being rude. Cook the man a meal of real food, and give him some lovin'.**

Be joyful, peaceful, gentle, meek, longsuffering, and full of faith. Don't just focus on your needs, and what you're not getting; instead become an expert at giving him what he needs. Sow seeds of love in him and you will reap the same. God determines what you will reap, either you believe His Word, or you don't.

Position Yourself to Receive

The Bible states in Hosea 10:12: *"Sow to yourselves in righteousness, reap in mercy; break up your fallow ground: for it is time to seek the Lord, till he come and rain righteousness upon you. Ye have plowed wickedness, ye have reaped iniquity; ye have eaten the fruit of lies, because thou didst trust in thy way, in the multitude of thy mighty men. Therefore shall a tumult arise among the people?"*

Repent now for putting other things and folk before the Lord. We have all done it, but you want to receive from God, don't here? How do you break up your fallow ground? Repent, humble yourself, and determine to put your hope in God. Specifically, abandon your idols, return to the Lord, and cleanse your temple.

You are so precious to the Lord, my sister. He has been waiting so long to bless you. He wants so much to fill your empty places with more love than you can ever contain. His heart's desire is to heal you and bless you with so much love that you can in return become a vessel of love and healing for others.

Why don't you, right now, pray to your Father in Heaven who loves you.

Lord, I come acknowledging that I have put other people or things before You, and I repent. I want You to be my Savior but also the Lord of my life. As my Lord I will look to You for all of my needs. You have promised to supply them according to Your riches in glory. I believe that in Your presence there are pleasures forever more. In Your presence is the fulfillment I need. Only You can touch my spirit, Lord. I yield unto You, I renounce all the lies of the enemy, and I bind the devil and every spirit of depression, hopelessness, fear, unbelief, and despair. I choose to walk in the joy of the Lord for it is my strength, not my emotions or fears, but I trust You to meet my need.

I offer myself to, You, Lord, as a living sacrifice, wholly, and acceptable to You, and even as I covenant to spend quality time in Your presence, I am available to be a vessel of healing and love for others. Thank You, Father. In the name of Jesus, I pray. Amen.

Discussion Questions
for Each Chapter

Chapter 1:

1. Why is it important to know what God thinks about women and His original plan for them?

2. What negative messages have you picked up as a woman? Where did they come from?

3. Have they impacted you?

Chapter 2:

1. How would you describe the Helpmeet?

2. How have you been a helpmeet to the men in your life?

3. What are some of the powers of influence that you have seen women use?

Chapter 3:

1. One of the main purposes of a wife is _____

    _____

    _____

    _____

2. What do you think would have happened if God had not made the changes in the relationships between Adam, Eve and Satan?

3. Have you experienced Satan's hatred for women or seen it in the world?

4. Have you ever identified your own hatred for Satan? (Just think about how you feel when someone bullies or hurts your children.)

5. When have you seen evidence that women's desire is towards their husband?

6. Since the husband's desire is not toward the woman, when and how do you see indication of an imbalance between the desires of men and women?

Chapter 4:

1. Can you think of a time or situation when you used any of these powers?

2. What ways have you influenced the males in your family or co-workers?

3. Can you think of a time when you used your influence in a negative way?

Chapter 5

1. Could you identify with any of the negative forms of communication discussed in the chapter?
2. What steps will you take to change that behavior?
3. Have you had experience with any of the negative forces of the tongue?
4. Have you experienced any of the positive forces of the tongue?
5. What steps will you take to make the Word of God more a part of you?

Chapter 6

1. Do you believe that God can use women spiritually to impact the world?

2. How do you deal with those Christians who believe women are to be seen and not heard?

3. How can the power of women be used in a negative way?

Chapter 7

1. Have you met any women operating to any degree on these levels of deception?

2. Have you ever been in a relationship with a person who was controlling? How did it make you feel?

3. Have you been or seen others under the negative influence of another?

4. Do you recognize yourself in any of the levels of deception?

5. What will you do to change the direction you are walking?

Chapter 8

1. What areas of weakness are hindering your life?

2. What do you do when you are criticized by others?

3. Do you ever have a hard time accepting the forgiveness of God?

4. Do you ever think about standing before God to answer for what you have done in this life? How do you think you are doing?

Chapter 9

1. Have you seen any evidence of the more subtle forms of rebellion in yourself?

2. What were the times and situations that trigger an overt rebellious reaction in you?

3. How do you feel when you are rebelling?

4. What are some of the consequences you have experienced when you rebelled?

5. Do you see yourself as a soldier in the army of the Lord? Are you skillful with your armor and your weapons?

Chapter 10

1. Have you had any hard experiences that taught you a good lesson or helped you to grow?

2. How does tribulation work patience? Have you experienced this?

3. What can you do to increase your trust in God?

Chapter 11

1. What are some of the problems you have seen women in leadership deal with?

2. How do you keep a positive attitude towards men when you deal with sexism?

3. Share any positive experience you have had with men that you were leading, teaching or supervising.

Chapter 12

1. Do you ever feel dry and empty sometimes?

2. Have you ever had any interesting worship experiences?

3. Have you ever sensed the presence of God around you? When and how does it make you feel?

4. Have you ever felt afraid of God's presence?

Chapter 13

1. Are you aware of times when you were leaning on and looking to something or someone else for your purpose and direction in life?

2. Have you ever been disappointed by someone you were counting on?

3. Have you found the secret place? If so, how did you find it? If not, what will you do to find it?

"The ministry of Clarence & Ja'Ola Walker is uniquely different, very powerful and soul liberating" –Babbie Mason, Recording Artist Atlanta Ga.

"They evidence a rare commitment for ministry. Few people give so much to the cause of Christ. They are well trained and effective, but it is their commitment that makes them special." – Dr. Tony Campolo, National speaker, author, professor. St. David, Pa

About the Author

―ᘒᘒ―

D r. Ja'Ola Walker is indeed a saved woman of virtue. She received an Honorary Doctorate of Divinity from Jameson Christian College, a M.Ed. in Counselor Education from West Chester State College and a BA in Psychology from Eastern College. (Now Eastern University) She received additional training from the Minnesota Institute for Couples Communication and Certified Parents Skills Inc. Dr Ja'Ola is the Co-Pastor of the Fresh Anointing Christian Center and a featured speaker at many conferences and seminars for women. She is a contributing author to the book, CALLED TO LEAD, and has served as an adjunct professor at Eastern Baptist Seminary. (Now Palmer Seminary) More importantly, she is a wonderful wife, dedicated mother and loving friend and prayer partner. She combines the anointing with beauty and class.

She had developed a set of teaching CD's that can be purchased on the website. www.clarencewalkerministries.com

Titles Like;

Wounded Women to Warrior Women
How to Talk to a Black Man
God's Way To Get a Man
Satisfaction Guaranteed
Build Baby Build
Reclaim God's Destiny for Your Royalty
Single: Preparation for Life